Praise for *Her Voice in Law*

"Rena Cook helps women lawyers bridge the gap between having book smarts and being a valuable team member, and becoming an independent, successful attorney who achieves excellent results for her clients. Women lawyers have to work harder and overcome innate challenges to achieve what male lawyers achieve naturally. Rena shows us how to do it effectively by teaching us how to use our voices and presentation skills to complete our skill sets. I recommend her instructions and advice to anyone who wants to excel as a trial lawyer."

—Melissa Dorman Matthews, Partner, Hartline Barger LLP

"As a solo practitioner for the last five years, this book really resonated with me. The insights on selling your services and networking are particularly spot on and practical! A valuable resource for entrepreneurs at any stage of their career."

—Jamie Miller, J Miller Law Firm PLLC

"This book is a must for any female attorney planning on entering a courtroom. As discussed in the book, a female attorney comes under closer scrutiny the second she steps foot in a courthouse. We inevitably feel that pressure, making us more anxious and unsure. The training, exercises, and advice given in this book help us overcome those insecurities so that we can find our powerful voices. I personally have worked with Rena on several occasions and am always mesmerized by how much of a difference the simplest exercise can have on not only my voice, but on my confidence. I am so excited that she and Laurie have brought these techniques to the masses."

—Kathleen Egan, Bundy Law Office

"Female? Male? Other? No matter. Your self-confidence, juror confidence in you and your case, and how seriously judges and jurors take you, all determine the trajectory of your cases and of your career. These essentials are mostly determined by how you sound. That's why *Her Voice in Law* instantly joins my list of the top ten trial advocacy books. In usable and concrete ways, it teaches and coaches you in the sine qua non of persuasion: finding and using your voice, which shapes how jurors interact with all else. And it's learnable for everyone. But men: ignore the title. Most of your women colleagues will read this book and soon do better than you; *Her Voice in Law* is your chance to keep up. Back in my theater days I saw that the success of almost all actors was directly proportional to the quality of their vocal coaches. This is even truer for trial advocates, and *Her Voice in Law* is a top-level vocal coach. So A+ to and gratitude for it. We've waited too long. After all, the root of the word 'ad<u>voc</u>ate' is not 'law' or 'strategy' or 'argument.' It's 'voice.'"

—David Ball, Author of *On Damages*

"What stands out about this publication is the way it lays out a comprehensive functionality of use for the reader. In its practical step-by-step, reader-focused process, it addresses a range of indispensable voice and presentation issues that are highly relevant for the female attorney in the contemporary workplace. In the light of ongoing gender inequity, the clear and robust remediation process outlined has the potential to effect positive workplace transformation for many of the thousands of women who seek to build meaningful and successful careers in the law and elsewhere. By setting the work within a transparent and attainable frame, this must-have text sets goals that are both realistic and attainable. With its ideas firmly rooted in the ground of what is possible, it says, above all, that change is within reach."

—Jane Boston, Leader MA/MFA Voice Studies:
Teaching and Coaching, Principle Lecturer,
The Royal Central School of Speech and Drama

HER VOICE IN LAW

RENA COOK AND LAURIE KOLLER
Illustrated by Carey Hissey

HER
VOICE
IN LAW

Vocal Power and Situational
Command for the Female Attorney

AMERICANBARASSOCIATION

ABA Publishing

Printed in the United States of America.

24 23 22 21 20   5 4 3 2 1

Library of Congress Control Number: 2020900467

Discounts are available for books ordered in bulk. Special consideration is given to state bars, CLE programs, and other bar-related organizations. Inquire at Book Publishing, ABA Publishing, American Bar Association, 321 N. Clark Street, Chicago, Illinois 60654-7598.

www.shopABA.org

Laurie and Rena dedicate this book to all the courageous women attorneys who are striving for justice, fighting for their clients, and winning the battle for equality. We stand on the strong shoulders of the women who came before and offer ours for the women who will come after.

Contents

Acknowledgments

No one works in a vacuum, especially on a project like this. Many people contributed to this book—to them we owe heartfelt gratitude.

Rena: I would like to thank my treasured voice and speech mentors who had deep and generous pockets: David Carey, Jane Boston, Rocco DalVera, Leslie Ann Timlick, Patsy Rodenburg, Kristin Linklater, Bonnie Raphael, and Gillyanne Keyes. Laurie: I would like to thank Don Keenan, David Ball, Louise Lipman, and Lexlee Overton for encouraging me along life's unfolding path.

We are deeply grateful to the following contributors: the inspiring attorneys whose stories, experiences, and advice appear in the Sidebars: Gale Allison, Beverly Atteberry, Shena Burgess, Jenny Proehl-Day, Stephanie Duran, Valerie Evans, Laura Clark Fey, Carly Hotvedt, Brittany Littleton, Rebecca Newman, Kathleen Pence, Lisa Riggs, and Esther Sanders. We also thank women leaders from numerous professional fields committed to women's empowerment: Anna Fearheiley, Cheena Pazzo, Diana Morgan, Teri Aulph, Aurora Gregory, Kathy Taylor, Felicia Collins Correia, and Ellen McClure.

Many people in the legal world supported us with advice and use of venues: Judge Linda Morrissey, GableGotwals, and Koller Trial Law. We also thank the mentors, trainers, authors, and friends who shared their time and expertise: Eliza Jane Schneider of Competitive Edge Voice Training; Ed Brodow, author of *Negotiations Boot Camp*; Robert Johnson of BoldNetworking.com; Michelle Lopez-Rios, Professor of Voice at De Paul University and former paralegal; and Matthew Ellis, Movement Specialist; actors supporting our attorneys in photos: Molly McBride Rogers, Patrick Hobbs, John Orsulak, Okcate Evita Smith, Steven McCommas, Julia Richards Bishop, Guy Black, Dan Call, Kenettha Ray,

Troy Cope, David Crass, Kim Rutherford, Elizabeth Buchner, and Latoya Rose; the ladies who inspired the illustrations: Jade Latimer Graham, Markeida Johnson, Erin Weaver, and Robin Rogers; our local team of readers, copy editors, transcribers, and technical support: Karen O'Brien, Pat Mitcho, Laualee Dick, Natalie Andrews, and Cherelle Demps. And final thanks to John Palmer at the American Bar Association as well as Donna King and her talented staff at Progressive Publishing Services.

Introduction

Self-assured speakers command our attention with their conviction, not their arrogance. They speak to higher principles and for the greater good but do so in a genuinely humble manner. Projecting self-assuredness is not about positioning yourself as "the expert," meeting perfectionist standards, or allowing the ego to run wild. Arrogance, flawlessness and dogmatism are merely the illusions of self-assuredness.

—Christine Jahnke[1]

Voice: Why Does It Matter?

One hundred years after they won the right to vote, women are owning their power in ways and in numbers they never have before. It is long past time for women in law to step forward, claim their vocal authority, and take their places as partners and lead counsel in numbers equal to those of their male counterparts. Even though social attitudes and cultural norms are evolving more rapidly now than in previous times, for the female attorney, change still happens slowly. The patriarchy in the legal system is especially entrenched due to centuries of tradition, protocol, and procedures. Precedent rules, and the precedent holds that men are in charge. Lara Bazelon, in her article in the *Atlantic,* confirms: "For the past two decades, law schools have enrolled roughly the same number of men and women. . . . In the courtroom, however, women remain a minority, particularly in the high-profile role of first chair at trial."[2]

In a 2017 study, the New York State Bar Association detailed the fact that "the low percentages of women attorneys appearing in speaking roles in courts was found at every level and every type of court."[3]

It was the dichotomy of the number of women entering the law compared with the number who stay and thrive that inspired Laurie Koller and me to collaborate on this book. Laurie, an attorney with almost thirty years' experience, specializes in civil representation for survivors of sexual assault, abuse, and injury. She came to me five years ago looking for voice training, with the goal of improving her vocal and physical communication in the courtroom. We have worked together ever since in a highly collaborative way. I share from the acting/voice/presentation perspective, and she educates me about specific demands placed on women in the law. Her mission as an attorney is to see her clients grow past and through the trauma they have endured. She wants to make sure her clients are armed with the resources to recover and heal. My mission is to help clients use their voices and bodies to tell their story, in confident and compelling ways, both in and out of the courtroom.

The Wall Street Journal reported in 2013 that "the sound of a speaker's voice matters twice as much as the content of the message."[4] In 350 BC, when asked to reveal the secret to his oratorical greatness, Demosthenes responded, "Delivery, delivery, delivery!" It may seem counterintuitive that *how* you say it matters more than *what* you say. To clarify this point, I conducted an informal experiment to see how much of an impact voice has on potential professional success. I asked a group of women to stand in front of a panel of observers. Each panel member was given a form on which they were to rank, on a scale of 1 to 5, each woman's look of trustworthiness and leadership potential: specifically, who looked like they would inspire trust and be an effective leader. The first ranking was taken on appearance alone, without voice. Then each woman spoke from a brief script. The panel was asked to rank again. Based on voice alone, some women went way up on the trustworthy/leadership potential scale and some went down. If the voice was pleasing or had gravitas, they were perceived by the panel to be more trustworthy with higher leadership potential, even if initially they did not have a "leader-like" look. If the voice was described as either childish or abrasive, they went down on the trustworthy/leadership scale.

Make no mistake, voice matters! People make judgments about us as soon as we open our mouths, as soon as we utter a word. Right or wrong, we are found to be educated or not, professional or not, calm and confident or not, hirable or not, believable or not. These assumptions are often formed solely on the quality of our voices and the clarity of our speech.

Voice quality can draw a jury in or push it away. A compelling, authentic, intelligible voice can get a jury on your side. A woman can lose power and weaken rapport if her vocal quality is strident, harsh, or nasal. She can sacrifice authority if words are not clear. She can lose credibility if volume is too low or too high or if the rate is too slow or too fast. A disconnect can occur when body language and gesture obscure the message. In a landmark 2001 report on sexism in the courtroom, Deborah Rhode, a Stanford Law professor, wrote that women in the courtroom face what she described as a "double bind . . . . Women . . . must avoid being seen as "too 'soft' or too 'strident,' too 'aggressive' or not 'aggressive enough.'"[5] However frustrated and perplexed we may be by these contradictions, we must move forward in productive and positive ways, dealing with the factors under our direct control—what is happening with our voices and bodies that may be keeping us from the success we desire and have trained for and deserve.

And trust us when we say there is a path between these seeming polar opposites that is neither too weak nor too strident, that is confident, strong, and authentic. Whatever the communication issue, this book will help you eliminate the barriers to power, authority, and expressivity.

Effective communication in and out of the courtroom is a challenge for both genders, and it goes back to the law school curriculum. Even in the finest law schools across the country, there are few classes on effective communication. A great deal of time is spent learning *what* to say but very little on *how* to say it. Unless a lawyer is a natural storyteller who instinctively knows how to keep an audience attentive, she may not know how to use voice and body language to win the jury's favor, sign a new client, or make a persuasive presentation. When so much is at stake, the very real edge that strong presentation skills offer can make the difference between a win or a loss.

You spend multiple hours and many days researching, writing, constructing, and rehearsing your argument in order to ensure success. If most attorneys follow this mode of preparation, why are some typically more effective than others?

In order to answer this question, I want to talk about a common human phenomenon. We, as human beings, love a good story. As was true of the ancient Greeks, who first took storytelling to a high art form, we love the drama and suspense of a great story. More specific to our task here, contemporary audiences are transfixed with courtroom dramas on both the large and small screen. We still love the drama. We can't resist a good "who done it" story—good versus evil, the little guy against capitalistic greed, the victim versus the perpetrator.

For our purposes, let's focus on a crucial element of any courtroom drama—the opening and closing statements, where, arguably, most litigators win or lose their cases. Accomplished screenwriters can create compelling and irresistible works of art through choice of word, arrangement of facts, attention to building suspense and delivery of the winning stroke at just the right moment. What do gifted screen-writers have that you don't? Is it a keener mind? Probably not. A better understanding of the law? Certainly not. Screenwriters hand their well-crafted words over to actors who understand the three dimensionality of storytelling and know how to bring the story to life through voice, emotions, and body language. An actor knows how to make us feel what they want us to feel, to see what they want us to see, to understand the truth from their character's point of view. Those of us who have had the privilege of serving on a jury might have said, "Well, it wasn't *Law and Order*," meaning it wasn't as exciting as TV. To which you may be tempted to say, "Well, it's not TV; it is real life and real life is sometimes pretty boring."

However, most of us will admit that the best storyteller frequently wins. The attorney who is comfortable and confident, who uses the voice in expressive ways, making a connection with the jury, client, or colleagues, is very likely to have an edge over the less expressive one.

LAURIE

As we begin to talk about presentation skills and effective storytelling in court, let me comfort you by saying there is a lot more bad out there than good. We, as women, often go into trial thinking everybody is better than we are.

In the teaching I have done, I have observed the average presentation ability is really quite low. Really fabulous lawyers—the ones fabulous in presentation and persuasion—have several factors in common. Variation of speed, rate, or tempo makes a huge impact. They consciously control how fast or how slow they talk. They are not afraid to use silence and slow pace. The default for most lawyers is to speak too fast and give too much information. The jury is quickly overwhelmed, and they stop listening. Finally, pitch variety has a huge impact: a fabulous litigator never speaks in a monotone.

Many lawyers adapt an inauthentic style I call "Mr. Lawyer Suit." You can sit down, talk to them over coffee, and they seem like normal human beings and you begin to build rapport. Then they stand up to present and it's like, who is this guy and where did he come from? They put on this suit of "Now I am going to be a lawyer." It gets the job done, but it doesn't do it well. It is not very per-suasive, and people tune out. Jurors can see through it; they know it's fake. The goal is to sound like a human being, a compelling persuasive human being. It is impossible unless you work on it. It seems counterintuitive that you have to work so hard to be authentic.

Laurie speaks of vocal traits that come under the umbrella of **expressivity**. Compelling an audience to attend to your words is not necessarily a talent you are born with. It is not an aptitude that you either possess or learn to live without. You can *learn* to be winningly expressive! I have trained actors most of my life, and I know that these skills can be taught. It is partly displaying ease and confidence. It is an ability to build suspense, using the voice and body in dynamic yet authentic ways. Through our work together in this book, you will learn how to take the words off the page to move a jury, convince an audience, spin a mystery, and keep the listeners on the edges of their seats. Whatever area of law is your specialty, there are specific skills which, with practice, can be mastered.

I started my career teaching high school drama before moving up to the college level. In the past two decades, I have focused on the voice, even taking a year off to get a Master's degree in Voice Studies. Recently, I have become fascinated by the real-life application of voice training. Though I love training actors, I have developed a passion for working with women attorneys and politicians—professionals who need to speak clearer, stronger, more authentically and expressively. It is deeply satisfying when, through our work together, someone's career prospects improve, their self-confidence grows and they are taken more seriously by their colleagues.

Through my training and consultancy business Vocal Authority, I have worked with a number of attorneys who have benefited from voice work and coaching in the areas of opening statements, closing arguments, examining witnesses, taking depositions, and securing new clients.

LAURIE

I've been an activist for women's issues since the '70 s when I was a small child. My mother and her friends were active and involved, so their conversations were always in the air. I soaked them up. I remember incidents of discrimination when I was a teenager. For example, I was into speech and debate, and I soon became indignant that girls' and boys' extemporaneous events were separate. Why was that? We couldn't compete with the guys?

When I got to law school, our class was the first to have more women than men. So I thought, oh great, we made it, right? We're done. Yeah, fat chance.

I first went to work for a large defense law firm that had three or four women partners, which was better than a lot of them frankly, but it wasn't anywhere close to half. The interview process, not just at that firm but at other firms, was discriminatory—there was a strong belief that women lawyers didn't belong in the courtroom. It was fine if you were a tax lawyer or wrote corporate documents. But there was no role for women in the courtroom.

That motivated me to want to excel in litigation. And when I did, I wanted to make sure other women had the chance to do that as well.

I've had success in jury trials in Oklahoma. I have a responsibility to make sure the women who are getting out of law school feel connected and believe they can succeed as well. I want to be an ally, provide a network of women they can reach out to, have lunch with, vent to. For me it was Sandra Day O'Connor. I'll never get to meet her, but I knew there was a woman lawyer out there. It gave me hope.

Women starting out now should see women attorney allies all around them. It's not just one shining woman on a hill. It is here and now. I've done the retreats and worked with Rena on this book in an attempt to normalize this kind of support network. We're closer to that point than we were thirty years ago. I have to believe thirty years from now will be even better.

My impulse to find Rena started years ago when David Ball gave the advice to find a voice coach. Not specifically to me, he said this to a seminar full of people. But it stuck in my head. I didn't know any voice coaches, and I didn't know how to find a voice coach, so it just remained a little nugget in the back of my head.

One day I was talking to my colleague David Bernstein who said he'd found a voice coach. "Oh my God, give me the number. I've been waiting for this." I followed up and connected with Rena. I discovered Lexlee Overton's work shortly after and recognized the synergistic effect of doing the voice work and the spiritual work. The meditation, the grounding, and the anti-anxiety strategies coalesce with the voice work, helping me achieve my professional goals without losing my mind. Finally, I am bringing it into the female development space; it all just belongs together.

In this book, Laurie and I have combined our areas of expertise to provide a comprehensive training for women attorneys who truly want to be better storytellers and more effective communicators.

How to Use This Book

Chapters 1 to 4 are organized around different aspects of the voice or body language, containing descriptions, definitions, and exercises. It is laid out in a sequential fashion, so it is best to work through the chapters as presented. Though you may be tempted to jump around, you will miss some vital information and foundational skill-based work that will ensure greater success and understanding.

Chapter 5 contains the application of the voice and body-skill work to the various legal settings within which you may be working.

When Laurie wants to speak directly to the reader, her words will appear in the gray box as seen below:

LAURIE

I need to say a few words in regards to preparation (which we will cover in detail later in the book). Work on the presentation skills as hard as you work on content. There was a time when we thought, "You are either born with a gift for storytelling or not. Here's your opening, go give it, we'll see what kind of skills you have." That's just wrong. Sure, some people are gifted in that area. But others can become fantastic storytellers with practice.

Much of our work will be practical. I will give you exercises that you can use to practice specific skills. I highly encourage you to do them. Just reading the narrative, explanations, and examples will not put the skills in your body ready to use in the pressure of the moment. Muscle memory is a powerful force and very challenging to change. If you truly want to become a more expressive attorney, you must practice, and practice some more, to retrain years of muscle memory. What your brain may learn in one read, your body may take months of repetition until it is comfortably authentic.

I will frequently ask you to be "aware" of what you feel, notice, or experience. Developing personal awareness is crucial as we exchange old habits for new. To that end, I encourage you to write about what you experience and learn from it. I have provided a place to journal, along with prompts to stimulate deeper reflection and encourage consistent practice. The very act of putting experiences into writing deepens the lessons and helps new and more effective behaviors take root, grow, and thrive.

The video is the "secret sauce." Use it! You can do the vocal warm up with me every day.

Each time this video icon ◾ appears, there is a video to demonstrate and guide the practice.

 Access the video at www.myvocalauthority.com/hervoiceinlaw. Enter the access code: HerVoiceinLaw1212.

Quotations from leading authors and researchers introduce the chapters, providing readers a glimpse into what others are saying about women, voice, and the law.

I interviewed successful women from across the country, both attorneys and other professionals. They shared stories, reflections, and advice about gender, voice, confidence, communication styles, and their relationships to success in the law. Their words place our work in a larger, real-world context. These amazing women gave me the gift of their time and open-heartedly shared their stories. Their inspiring contributions are featured under the Sidebar subheading. A bio of each woman can be found at the end of the book.

It is important to find an accountability partner or form a group of women attorneys who want real and lasting voice and presentation transformation. If you meet once a week, or bimonthly, and work through the process together, giving support and feedback, the vocal growth for each of you will soar. You can work through the process together—it is laid out for you to follow. A different member of the group can lead each session. Between the content outlined in the book and the video, you have all the tools you need.

For both Laurie and me the act of writing this book has clarified and deepened our commitment to making a difference in the lives of women lawyers who have been held back by solvable communication issues. All of us desire to be the best possible versions of ourselves; we long to communicate in the most compelling and inspiring ways. This book answers that need. It is my hope that the processes outlined here will help you enhance your voice and confidence so that you can ultimately achieve your goals in the courtroom, depositions, legal transactions, and within your firm or practice.

Sidebar

Early on, my career in law was greatly impacted by my gender. I started practicing in Washington, DC, in the '80s, so there weren't as many women lawyers as there are now. I'm so pleased that women are catching up. But it was very hard then to stake out your abilities in the courtroom, in depositions, even in phone conversations with clients who wondered if you could really be their champion. Could you really fight for them? Would you be strong enough? Would you be tough enough? Would you be effective enough as a woman to do what litigators do? It was fairly obvious that there were some prejudices against female litigators.

I had to put my head down and try to be the best I could be. I thought I had to prepare better, know my information better. That has eased up. As you develop confidence and hone your skills, you can relax some. It's always in the background, but as you establish your reputation, if you're good at what you do, people will trust they can count on you to do a good job. It has to be built with time, and that's true for men or women, frankly. But more so for women.

The women I admire and respect most have a quiet confidence, not overplaying any aspect. Women have to be very careful about that. I think men get away with raising their voices and being more dramatic than women can. There are a lot of labels that get thrown at women if you don't have certain boundaries with your voice, your presentation—steady, calm but confident, respectful and firm.

—Lisa Riggs, Attorney

Most women lawyers are going to face resistance and negative perceptions from time to time because of their gender. Women can choose to allow this to make them sad or angry. Or they can choose to view such negativity as a challenge—and focus their energy on proving people wrong in their perceptions, rather than on negative emotions that sap their energy and confidence.

My advice to new attorneys is to trust in yourself and your abilities. Push yourself to learn and do as much as you can as fast as you can. View it as an opportunity when someone underestimates you—you can definitely use that to your advantage. The practice of law is a relationship business—take time to really develop strong relationships—with your colleagues, with co-counsel, with opposing counsel, with judges, and all other business and personal contacts. Look for opportunities to help other women.

—Laura Clark Fey, Attorney

Chapter 1

Tuning Your Instrument

*I tell my female students the truth: that their body and demeanor
will be under constant scrutiny from every corner of the courtroom.
That they will have to pay close attention to what they wear and
how they speak and move.*

—Lara Bazelon[6]

A woman's voice, probably more than any other trait, elicits a great deal
of feedback, with the possible exception of her wardrobe. Through
awareness, training, and practice you can indeed turn what could
be a negative into a positive. In this chapter, you will begin to gain
flexibility so that your voice can adapt to your situational needs and
intentions, as well as the size of the space in which you are speaking.
In theatrical terms, this process would be called tuning your instrument because the voice and the body are truly the instruments you are
learning to play.

Understanding the voice is the first step. Your relationship with your
own voice is surprisingly complex. It is connected to the core of who
you are. It is linked to your past, your emotions, your motivations, your
desires, and your health. Your voice reveals your essence to the world.
Whether you are confident, secure, happy, healthy, inspired, or intim-
idated, your voice tells all. We often feel vulnerable when doing voice
work because it feels so personal. We have been speaking for almost as
many years as we have been alive, and now we are looking through a
microscope and attempting to change well-established patterns.

Most of us hate the sound of our own voice when we first hear it on a
recording. "I don't really sound that way, do I?" That is a normal, almost
universal reaction, and you need to get beyond that because you will be

listening to your recorded voice a lot—it is the best feedback you don't have to pay for.

We will start the vocal transformation with the foundational components and systematically scaffold a structure for success. This scaffold includes training the voice and body to work together in a complex integration of multiple systems. Like any musical instrument, it must be tuned each time it is played, so that all parts are functioning optimally. In this chapter, we break it down system by system. The process may feel slow the first time through. Once the sequence is taught and understood, however, it can go fairly quickly. In as little as fifteen minutes a day, you can gain flexibility and control of your instrument.

Take a moment to think of a compelling attorney who shines easily and authentically in front of a jury. It can be an attorney you have seen in actual practice or one from film or television. Let's call this lawyer the "litigator from heaven." What specific qualities do such litigators display? Think in terms of voice, body, and emotions, of how they make you feel.

Excellent expressive litigators usually have a number of qualities in common, namely:

- They have an easy confidence—not forced, pressed, defensive, or combative, but unwavering and authentic.
- Their voices are strong and clear, easily heard and understood.
- They are comfortable in their own skins; they can stand easily and be still.
- They know what to do with their hands. When they move or gesture, the action carries specific meaning and has an impact that clarifies intention.
- They make eye contact to share and shift the jury's focus.

These are the descriptors I generally hear first, and they provide us with great starting points.

Let me challenge you to observe your litigator from heaven more deeply. Let's start with a property of the voice that is easily observable and that for women is a major focus of criticism—**pitch**, which is the relative highness or lowness of the voice in terms of notes on a musical scale. Think about **pitch range** as a continuum from the highest note a person can comfortably speak to the lowest. What do you notice about the pitch of the voice of your litigator from heaven? Expressive storytellers usually speak in the middle of their range, neither staying too high nor settling too low. You will also notice that more of the pitch range is in use. A monotone voice that is speaking on one or two notes rapidly grows old (think about your most boring law school professor).

Another vocal characteristic that draws much focus for the woman in law is her quality or tone. Recall again the voice of your litigator from heaven. We are listening to how the voice sounds and how it makes us feel. Tone, or quality, is created by **resonance**. The expressive attorney has a variety of tonal qualities that elicit various emotions from the listener.

Let's shift our observational focus to **rate** and **rhythm**: how fast or slow does the ideal litigator speak? My guess is that the litigator from heaven uses a variety of speeds. Some sentences are delivered pretty quickly, while some phrases or even single words are given more length and are spoken more slowly.

The **volume** of the expressive voice, how loud or soft, never falls below what everyone in the courtroom can hear. Nor does it go beyond the level of comfortable projection. If we talk about volume on a scale of one to ten, one being the softest and ten the loudest, the expressive attorney's volume will move between three and eight. This is a lot of variety at our disposal without ever getting too soft or too loud.

In terms of body language, some lawyers are too uncertain to move at all, while some never stop moving. Both of these physical landscapes are distracting because such movement does not contribute to overall communication. The expressive litigator does not move around too much and uses gestures or movement only when needed to communicate or reinforce a specific point—I need the jury to look at me, not at the defendant, so I move closer to the jury; I want the jury to watch only the victim, so I move close to her. Too much nervous movement distracts from the message. In the eyes and ears of the audience, movement will always take precedence over the spoken word.

Before we go any further, I want to make something clear. The expressive attorney is never "over the top," pushy, off-putting, or strident—labels that are too often ascribed to attorneys, especially women. No one deliberately trains to be that person. Rather, the truly compelling, believable lawyer is comfortably authentic, easy, flexible, clear, and engaging. Who doesn't want to be that litigator? Our mission is to help you be a more authentic and compelling truth teller.

Why Women Lose Their Voices

Stand in the middle of an elementary school playground and hear children raising their voices in play. If you cover your eyes, you won't be able to tell the difference between the boys and the girls. They shout, command, rejoice, get angry, share, reject, lead, and follow. All children sound the same.

Stand in the hall in a junior high school, and you hear a different sound. Boys are louder, girls are softer; and it is not just because of the biology of boys' voices developing. New rules, spoken and implied, are made evident to both girls and boys by teachers, parents, peers, and the media, which define acceptable behavior and voice. Boys are encouraged to be independent, to speak up, and to lead. Girls historically have been encouraged to "tone it down." To be popular, girls have to be less vocal, less loud, and less bossy—girls have to be less. While boys are typically praised for assertive behaviors both at play and in the classroom, girls are frequently admonished for the same behaviors.

For many girls, the energy and authentic confidence voiced in childhood go into hiding. To maintain harmony, we learn to keep up the illusion that we are perfect little ladies; we learn to contain the voice. Carol Gilligan, in her book *In a Different Voice*, writes: "[M]any women feared that others would condemn them or hurt them if they spoke, that others would not listen or understand, that speaking would only lead to further confusion, that it was better to appear 'selfless,' to give up their voices to keep the peace."[7] We learned these lessons early, and for many of us the patterns of deferring, speaking softly, letting our actions speak for us, compromising, or accepting less can stay with us for a lifetime.

Now skip ahead a couple of decades and we notice that the behaviors that were rewarded by teachers, parents, and peers don't serve us in the courtroom or within our law firms. Professionals who advance to the highest levels speak up, make decisions quickly, think and act independently, and confidently tell their clients' stories. Those of us who have played by the "perfect little girl" rules find ourselves at a distinct disadvantage.

For other young girls, the authentic voice hides in a different direction. The fear of not being taken seriously, the need to be heard, or the pain of an abusive home can lead to overcompensating with too much energy, pressing, and stridency. Flexibility, vulnerability, and humanity get frozen out. Alignment becomes rigid as the woman armors herself to withstand the forces that can harm her. This extreme does not work well, either.

Grounding and Centering

When a girl or a young woman suppresses her voice for any reason, her voice will go to one of two default settings. First, it may go into hiding, staying soft, quiet, childlike, and self-deprecating. I call this **Denial**.[8] We all know this gal—her voice is thin and soft, unsupported by breath, choked in the throat. We notice that her shoulders are slightly rounded, that the head hangs forward. Her voice has caved in on itself. She may receive feedback like "You don't really command authority." "You don't take charge." "You seem tentative." "You are just not leadership material."

The second default setting is at the other extreme: **Bluff**. This is the default setting of the woman who projects the idea that "If I am going to succeed in a man's world, then I will walk and talk like a man!" Her voice is strident, aggressive, or pressed, her shoulders are drawn back, her chest is high, and her chin is lifted. She may frequently get criticism such as "You come on too strong." "You seem angry all the time." "You intimidate people." "You're bossy." She presses out of habit or because she fears she is not enough, so she tries extra hard.

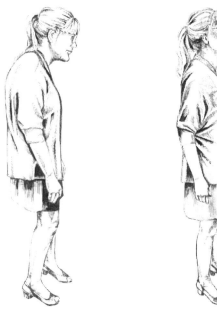

Denial Posture   **Bluff Posture**

These examples—Denial and Bluff—are obviously two extremes. And frankly, in my life, I have exhibited both in different situations. The **authentic voice** lies between Denial and Bluff, the place in our bodies where we can find power without press. We are comfortably strong, we are easily confident, we are powerful without having to press for it. The authentic voice lives in the **grounded, centered**, easy body. It is only from a place of ease that we can access our true power, the place from which our voice is strong, clear, and compelling.

Exercise: Denial versus Bluff

For this exercise you will need a simple personal introduction statement that includes your name, your firm, and your practice specialty. Write it out so you don't have to worry about word choice.

- Stand in your **familiar** way, the way you always stand. Don't judge or change it; just bring awareness into your body. Be aware of your head and neck, where your shoulders are, where your hips are, where your weight is distributed over your feet.
- In your familiar stance, introduce yourself using the introduction statement. Without judging, be aware of how that sounds and feels.
- Now allow your shoulders to round forward, slump a little, your head comes forward, your pelvis settles back. This is the Denial stance. As you stand in this way, certain feelings or thoughts may start to flow, "I am not prepared. I am not ready. Everyone else is better than I am."
- In Denial, say your introduction statement. Be aware of your voice now. What does it sound and feel like?
- Still standing, draw your spine up long and tall, pull your shoulders back, stretch across your chest, lift your chin. This is the Bluff stance. Now say your introduction. How do you sound and feel now?
- Now adjust your stance. Relax your shoulders so that they are down a bit but not drooping forward. Feel the long back of your neck and the soft front of your neck, position your chin parallel to the floor, move your feet so that they are a hip-width apart and your weight is evenly distributed. This is your **natural stance**. Say your introduction again. Is this different? What does the voice sound like? What do you think it conveys?

    In this simple exercise, we went from familiar alignment to denial to bluff to natural. When coming from this natural stance—balanced, upright, but not rigid or held—your authentic voice is powerful without press or effort.

Grounding

We use the term **grounding** when we speak of our stability, our foundation, which starts with our feet. The feet must always be in solid contact with the floor. A sense of gravitas, the quality that projects inner confidence, comfort, and quiet power, is built on this foundation—an awareness that the feet are connected to the floor, drawing energy up from the earth.

- Stand in the natural way we experienced earlier—long back of neck, soft front of neck. Place your feet hip-width apart, toes pointed straight ahead, and soften your knees. Imagine that the base of the big toe, the base of the little toe, and the heel form a solid triangle of support. Keeping the knees released, stand firmly on that triangular base and relish the sense of strength it gives you.

- Rock forward on your toes, then back on your heels several times. Rock side to side across the bottom of your feet. Find that place where the weight is evenly balanced over both feet. Imagine the bones in the foot spreading out across the floor.
- Feel as though you can draw energy and support from the earth. Imagine that energy is drawn up through the soles of the feet, that the whole of the earth is supporting your body as it speaks and moves.
- Speak your introduction statement, enjoy feeling the sound coming up through your body from your grounded base.

Centering

If grounding has to do with feeling the feet against the floor, **centering** has to do with the awareness that your power center is just below the navel. Place your hand on your lower abdomen and imagine that all your thoughts, opinion, emotions, and experiences are housed in your center, under your hand. When we are pressing, the energy goes high in the chest as the chin juts forward to prove a point. When we speak weakly or breathily, the energy dissipates before our words can leave our mouths. If we shift that focus to our center and imagine that the center is leading us through space or guiding our thoughts and inspiration, it puts our power lower in the body where it is more effective and reliable.

- Stand with feet hip-width apart, knees relaxed, shoulders down, long back of neck, soft front of neck. Feel the grounding of your feet, the energy coming up through the floor. Place a hand just below your navel. Focus on your center. Imagine the video of your mind, which is playing in your head all the time, is actually located in your center. It is like a camera lens that is not at eye level but at your center.
- Envision a hoped-for accomplishment: delivering the perfect opening or closing, expressing the perfect thought at a meeting, adeptly steering a deposition to the desired outcome. Turn on the video camera in your center and see it happening there—not in your mind's eye but in your belly.
- Now speak your introduction statement from this place of powerful awareness. Be aware of how little effort you need from the waist up if you are grounded and centered.

Powering without Pressing

*We must continue to develop the ability to stand unapologetically
in our power as a woman, or as an attorney, or as a professional,
or as a mother, wife. Be proud that you have ambitions. In my
community of women, solo practitioners who have left more
traditional law firms, what motivates us, whether we can verbalize
it initially or not, is a rejection of the power dynamic found in
the traditional law culture. Our perception of what it means to
be powerful is having to climb over other people, and there's an
inherent violence in that. Even if it's not physical, it's kind of an
emotional violence. I reject that.*

—Brittany Littleton, Attorney

Power without Press

Many successful attorneys, speakers, leaders, and politicians come to
me with a common, often insidious problem. They find their power
through pressing—through working too hard in the wrong parts of the
body. When I see shoulders pressed back, chests coming forward, and
chins lifting, I know what kind of sound I am going to hear—shouting,
grating, abrasive, forced, or husky. This approach will never be ultimately effective because it is not authentic, not inviting, not convincing,
and it will always prove to be vocally fatiguing to the person speaking.

Hillary Clinton is a perfect example. On the campaign trail, when she wanted to rally her crowds, her voice went into overdrive, shouting and pressing. Audiences tire of this type of delivery pretty quickly. Juries, potential clients, and colleagues pick up on this immediately and find it off-putting.

Instead, I teach women to relocate their center of power to the lower abdomen. This way of thinking is about how energy is produced and how it emanates from your body. Most people think that in order to show power they have to press from the upper chest. The shoulders lock back, the chin goes up, and they are "off to the races," but not in a good way. If you release habitual tension in the body, ground and center, and feel the breath deep in your torso, you will find an easier, yet stronger, source of power. When you want to "dial up" power or volume, focus on engagement in your center. The rest of the body, particularly the shoulders, head, and neck, stay released.

Exercise: Power without Press

- Give each foot a good shake. Ground and center yourself as you did in the previous exercise.
- Soften your knees and feel your neck lengthening.
- Breathe slowly and deeply.
- Say "ha" through a big, easy, open mouth.
- With each new breath, say "ha" again, each time feeling a little more engagement from your abdominals. Feel a little pulse in your belly on each sound. It is as if you are dialing up the energy, one notch at a time, without tensing anywhere else in the body. Stop when you begin to feel the throat tensing up.
- On a new breath, say a big open "hello." Feel engagement in your center. Check your neck and shoulders to make sure they stay loose and free. Let the sound roll out of a big open mouth. Try the word "tomorrow" in this same way. Then say, "tomorrow and tomorrow and tomorrow," feeling the power from your abs while keeping the shoulders and neck free.

As we build on these beginning exercises, you will become more and more acquainted with the "power without press" feeling. This is always where we start and where we return—it is our touchstone for all the work that follows.

Staying grounded and centered isn't easy; it takes practice and daily attention. On the days that I feel shaky and uncertain, I am comforted by the words of Leila Janah, founder and chief executive of Samasource: "You have to be willing to embrace the struggle. If you want anything great in life, you have to be willing to go through the dark and painful moments of building something. Nothing great has ever come out of the easy days . . . only through struggle is our character really tested."[9] And with practice, every day, we can stay present and grounded so that we are better able to confront the challenges with clear, strong, authentic voices.

Video #1: Denial, Bluff; Grounding, Centering, Power without Press
(Access the video at www.myvocalauthority.com/hervoiceinlaw. Enter the access code: HerVoiceinLaw1212.)

Reflective Journal

Record what you experienced as you worked through the Denial/ Bluff exercises. Did one exercise feel more familiar to you? What did you hear or feel in your voice as you moved between these default stances? What did a natural, authentic stance feel like by contrast? What are your thoughts about grounding? At what point did you feel the most change or shift? Where in the body are you most aware of change? What is happening with the breath? Have your feelings or emotions shifted at all? How did your voice change as you shifted your source of power to your center?

_____

_____

_____

_____

_____

_____

_____

Sidebar

Among my young colleagues, I observe two kinds of behavior. Some behave in what I think of as immature, flighty, giggly, overly aware of wardrobe choices that heighten femininity. I want to tell those women that it really hurts their credibility in this field because you're automatically deemed not smart or serious—which may not be true, but that's how it comes off. Then on the flip side are the women who are much more serious, who are judged as aggressive. And so whatever you do, you're damned if you do; you're damned if you don't. I have been told I'm too aggressive, when I think I am just being assertive. When a man is aggressive, he is seen as wise, strong, a leader. But when a woman is aggressive, she is labeled bitchy and emotional.

Successful women that I want to emulate hold themselves up. They don't slouch; they own their space. They don't demand attention or beg for attention, but they don't shy away from it either. They are who they are. They are comfortable with themselves, they have a sense of power in themselves. And a woman's voice is attached to how much power she has. The most persuasive female voices I have heard are strong and commanding, but not abrasive. They are never meek, which would be perceived as a weakness. However, if you are yelling and being overly loud, then you come off overly aggressive.

—Kathleen Pence, Attorney

When I fall into one of these traps, it will be "Bluff" every time. I spent years unlearning my physical rigidity. Certain vocal and physical tactics have helped me establish a genuine, confident presence without leaning into "Bluff." I can be grounded without having my feet glued to the floor. I give myself the freedom to move with purpose through a room at key points in a presentation. And as someone with a naturally louder voice, I have power without having to push for it; it was all about relaxing enough to let my breath do the work.

One of our many challenges as women at work is the pressure (whether internal or external, real or imagined) to be simultaneously feminine, sexy, maternal, funny, and a trustworthy, competent leader. Traits that are stereotypically "sexy" (soft voice, soft gestures, artful glances) are opposed to the recipe for confident, authentic communication. Some habits we may have accidentally picked up along the way must first be broken down to make room for new skills. If power without press feels inauthentic at first, give it a few weeks of practice. Soon you'll find yourself armed with an aligned posture and a stronger, healthier voice—suddenly, communicating with these tools becomes natural because it's your body's favorite state of being!

—Anna Fearheiley, Theatre Producer, Administrator

The women I have worked with, and I have found this to be true in myself, are less likely to press or be forced when they are confident. When we are settled in our minds that we are the one who should be talking because we have the expertise and the experience, we all tend to relax. We get to be more of our authentic selves, with less tension. I see less caving in, "denial" as you call it, as well as less "bluffing," pushing to be like a man. With confidence comes relaxation, authenticity and presence.

—Aurora Gregory, Author, Trainer

I had witnessed women who just pushed their way in, like a bulldozer, with a chip on their shoulder; as if someone was trying to take advantage of them. With that kind of demeanor, what they are actually communicating is they don't belong there. I was determined to hold my own without ever being rude. I believed that if I were gracious, true to myself, and held my own that I wouldn't ever have to be that way.

—Teri Aulph, Leadership Trainer

Releasing Habitual Tension

Leaders take charge, but a woman with a dominant style can be viewed as too abrasive or pushy. The glass ceiling is cracked, but women still wage battle against sexism, low self-esteem and stage fright . . . the male voice still dominates the public square. As long as women remain a vocal minority in corporate boardrooms, on TV talk shows, and in the halls of Congress, we pay a price for being voiceless. The world needs well-spoken women to state opinions in every venue from PTA meetings to presidential debates.

—Christine K. Jahnke[10]

Social Science research has demonstrated that when female attorneys show emotions like indignation, impatience, or anger, jurors may see them as shrill, irrational, and unpleasant. The same emotions when expressed by men are interpreted as appropriate to the circumstances of the case.

—Lara Baselon[11]

A young female attorney stands before a group of potential jurors. It is her job to conduct the voir dire, a very crucial first step toward a winning verdict. She knows her client and colleagues are depending on her. Thousands of dollars hang in the balance, as well as her reputation as a capable member of the team. Going through her mind is the question, "Oh God, why did I ever think I could do this? I am going to crash and

Tense Alignment

burn. There is no way." She feels a knot in the pit of her stomach, her shoulders draw closer to her ears, her breath is rapid and shallow, and her knees are locked. When she opens her mouth to speak, the sound is barely audible, not like it sounded during the focus group session. Her face flushes, her knees begin to quiver.

Does any of this sound at all familiar?

Tension murders the voice! The inner critic, with her endless litany of negative mental messages, causes tension, which murders the voice. Tension anywhere in your body will shut down the voice, shut down the breath, shut down connection to your authentic spontaneous self, and shut down your ability to be fully present. We have all fallen victim to this phenomenon. In that moment, it feels as if we are at the mercy of our bodies and these responses are beyond our control.

Let me pose a question. Does the body follow emotion, or does emotion follow the body? Like the chicken-or-the-egg analogy, it is actually both. Emotions go where the body goes, and the body goes where the emotions go. In my work with actors, I have found it is easier to control the body than it is to control the emotions, so my daily practice, which includes my warm-up ritual, always begins with the body. Although I acknowledge that tension is the inevitable by-product of living in a modern world, it is the enemy of the authentic, expressive voice and the freely moving body. Tension anywhere in the body stifles sound and muffles articulation. Learning how to release habitual tension is one of the first steps toward releasing a free, clear, and dynamic voice. By releasing tension, we find a state of "relaxed readiness."

The tension we normally carry in our bodies makes itself known through headaches, indigestion, muscle aches, joint pain, insomnia, and free-floating anxiety. We are aware of the physical toll that stress and tension create, but most of us are not aware of the price we pay in our voices. The vocal folds (also called vocal chords), which actually produce the sound, are small, delicate membranes in the larynx, no bigger than the size of a thumbnail. The weight of any tension in the body eventually radiates and finds its way to the folds, causing them to work harder than they should. Hidden little tensions like toes gripping the floor, locked knees, fixed pelvic girdle, rigid spine, tense arms, fingers, shoulders, neck, jaw, and tongue will eventually limit and stifle the voice.

Where does this tension come from? Just the fact that we, as human beings, walking upright in defiance of gravity, create tension as we move through the day. Each vertebra is pulled toward the earth, causing the spine to compress. The weight of the head, 12 to 14 pounds, is pulled forward. The shoulders move closer to the ear lobes, the back of the head sinks onto the top of the spine, the muscles that separate the ribs shorten, the chest falls toward the stomach, the knees lock, and the ankles tighten. With this collapsing of space in the body comes a collapse of the voice as well. The voice has less space in which to live, less space to gather energy and vibrancy, less resonance, less volume, and less brilliance. When space inside the body diminishes, the jaw, tongue, and vocal folds jump in to compensate, helping to push the voice. This compensation only creates more tension, tightness, and effort. The voice gets thin or strident and may feel scratchy and fatigued.

The simple activities of daily living—getting the kids off to school or arriving at work on time, performing well in a deposition, staying fit, pleasing the law partners or your spouse—all cause the body and the voice to tighten. While it is impossible to live in this world tension free, it is possible to soften the body and the breath, to let the jaw hang loose, and to relax the tongue away from the hard palate. These simple, specific adjustments throughout a stress-filled day can make a huge difference. Releasing tension is a constant commitment and a daily challenge, and it is crucial to achieving a strong, clear voice.

The three quickest and easiest ways to release tension from the body and create space for the voice are to stretch, shake, and breathe deeply. In the following exercises, we will do a little of each. As you work, focus each exhale on a gentle *fff* sound at your lips, and the inhale will take care of itself.

Exercise: Basic Relaxation Preparation

Start this sequence by creating a simple introductory paragraph of three to four sentences, including your name and a statement of what you are most passionate about, in either your practice or your private life. Write it down here.

_____

_____

_____

_____

     Always start voice work with some variation of the following basic exercise. It brings you to presence and shakes away tension so that the voice is free to work.

- Shake your hands.
- Shake one foot, then the other.
- Move your hips in a big circle.
- Roll your shoulders.
- Stretch up on your toes, arms reaching toward the sky.
- Sigh out a huge sound of relief.

 Video #2: Isolation of Body Parts; Internal Space Awareness, Spinal Roll
(Access the video at www.myvocalauthority.com/hervoiceinlaw. Enter the access code: HerVoiceinLaw1212.)

Exercise: Internal Space Awareness

In order for the voice to work most efficiently and effectively, a feeling of space must be continually created in the body: space in the mouth, space in the neck, space up the spine, space between the ribs, space between the shoulders and earlobes, space across the shoulder girdle, space in the joints, space in the torso, space in the lungs, and space in the abdomen. These naturally occurring spaces in the body collapse and get smaller as we pick up tension throughout the course of the day. Drawing awareness to inner space begins to free the voice as it relaxes the body. A quick note about volume and filling a large space: the larger the space, the more sense of inner space you need to carry within you.

As you work through this exercise, remember to breathe; imagine that you can breathe into the spaces you are creating. Close your eyes so that you can better envision the inside of the body.

- Stand with feet hip-width apart, knees released, and eyes closed.
- Think of the top of the head floating up as if filled with helium, the face forward, the back of the neck long. Imagine that your neck is growing skyward with the chin parallel to the floor.
- Feel the jaw relaxed and hanging loosely from the skull, with teeth slightly apart. Allow the tongue to rest on the floor of the mouth with the tip behind and gently touching the bottom teeth.
- Feel the weight of the shoulders giving into gravity; be aware of the distance between your shoulders and earlobes.
- Imagine a ball of energy moving out from the middle of the shoulders, widening and lengthening along the shoulders.
- Imagine that your upper arm is moving away from your shoulders, the lower arm is moving from your elbow, and your hands are moving away from your wrist.
- See your rib cage as a large, airy barrel surrounding your spine; imagine your lungs as two large balloons filled with air.
- Imagine that your spine is growing in two directions as the head floats to the sky, the tailbone toward the earth. Be aware of the space between the vertebrae.
- Be aware of the space between your hips and your torso. Imagine that the torso can move up and away from the hips.
- Feel the space between your thighs and shins.
- Imagine that the feet are spreading out against the floor.
- Relish how tall and light you feel as you find space inside the body; breathe into all the newfound spaces.
- With this new sense of inner space, breathe in and speak: count one through ten and say your introductory statement. Be aware of changes in your sound.

Throughout this work, I will remind you of the importance of creating the image of space within the body. This sensation is one you want to maintain as you do this vocal work. Even under the pressure of speaking in public, if you start to feel that the voice is not working just right, simply think space and your voice will right itself.

Exercise: Isolation of Body Parts

- Stand with your feet parallel, hip-width apart, with your weight evenly distributed over both feet.
- Let a breath drop into your body and sigh out a robust sigh of relief; this brings your mind and breath into the body. Sigh out several more times on voice: a hearty "ahh." With each sigh, feel a deeper sense of relief.

The **neck**, where the vocal folds are housed, is a huge repository of tension. The goal here is to maximize your sense of space in the back of the head and neck. Each of the release exercises below should be repeated with gentle-to-moderate effort at least ten times.

- Let your chin drop to your chest and shake your head "no." Be aware of the gentle pull between the shoulders.
- Let your right ear float near your right shoulder, and drop your chin forward onto the chest. Then let your left ear float to the left shoulder. Go back and forth as if you are inscribing a "happy face" in the air with the top of your head. It is rather like a "suspend and fall" movement—the movement of the head suspends over one shoulder, and then falls as the chin returns heavily to the chest and rolls up to the other side.
- Inscribe a circle in the air with the tip of your nose. Start with a small circle, then let it get larger. Reverse direction, going from large to small.
- Feel the top of the head floating up as if filled with helium; the sensation of "long back of neck, soft front of neck" is key and recurrent in the work. The face is forward and eyes are on the horizon as the back of the neck lengthens toward the sky. Be aware of the space between the head and shoulders and the space between the vertebrae in the neck.

The **shoulders** are a favorite spot for tension to collect. As I go through the day, I find my shoulders getting closer and closer to my earlobes. As I sit at the computer, listen to an animated client or a frustrated colleague, or answer a sales question, I can feel that space getting smaller and smaller. Follow the steps below to enhance the space above and below the shoulders. Ten repetitions is our magic number.

- Circle the shoulders slowly, putting all your concentration into a controlled perfect circle. Feel the shoulder joints getting looser and wider as the size of your circle increases. Breathe deeply as though you can lubricate the shoulders with breath. Reverse the circle.
- Bounce the shoulders gently, lifting them high to the earlobes and dropping them low and heavy.
- Swing one arm in a large circle like a windmill, first in one direction, then the other. Swing the other arm in the same way.

- Shake your hands by relaxing at the wrist and gently flapping up and down.

Torso and spine

A physical therapist once told me that you are only as healthy as your spine. Keeping the spine supple and flexible with these simple daily exercises is part of the process for the good of the voice and the good of your general health. The following sequence should be done with an awareness of creating space between ribs, space between vertebra, and a general openness and expansion of the torso.

- With arms loosely out from the body, gently twist your torso from side to side, increasing flexibility in the spine. This is a relaxed movement; do not throw your body from side to side, just let it go there.

Spinal Roll

- Roll down the **spine** slowly, feeling the head giving into gravity, one vertebra at a time, knees bent, head and arms remaining free all the way down. Shake out some sound, feeling it fall out the top of your head. Sigh out a deep sigh of relief. Roll up slowly from the base of the spine, again focusing on length and space. The neck and head are the last to come up. Be aware of the easy natural alignment of the spine, neck, and head as you come to standing position.

- **Ribs:** The ribs and the muscles between each rib encase the lungs. If they are stretched and released, the lungs can take a deeper, easier breath. To open the muscles between the ribs, reach your right arm over your head and stretch it toward the left. Keep your knees relaxed as you imagine breathing into your exposed rib cage; hold the stretch for five breaths. Imagine that you are "presenting the rib cage," as if showing that exposed rib cage to the world. Your arm remains up as you vigorously pat the rib cage. Let your arms relax at your side. Allow a deep breath to drop into your torso. Does the stretched side move more in response to the breath?

Rib Stretch

- Repeat this stretch and pat on the other side. When both arms return to your side, be aware of the sense of lift and expansion in the ribs. You have created more space for the lungs to inflate with air.

Lower body

From the waist down, including hips, pelvic girdle, knees, and ankles, we hold tension that we need to let go of.

- To release the hips and pelvic girdle and create a sense of inner space, move your hips in a big, sloppy circle, like working a hoola hoop, ten times in one direction and ten in the other. The knees stay released. Add an easy hum with your lips together, teeth apart. Open the sound to an "aah," letting the sound mirror the circle of the hips.

- Put a gentle shake in your hips to give a final loosening to the whole area. Add an easy "ahh" as you move.
- Lift your foot and circle at the ankle, first in one direction and then in the other. Think of a perfect circle in your ankle. Imagine that you can draw breath up through the sole of your foot. Repeat ten times in each direction with each ankle. Enjoy the space you have created between the foot and the rest of the leg. You can also add a hum as you circle the foot.

Through the above exercises, you have loosened the body, released some of the tension that blocks the voice, gently warmed up your voice, and created inner space that will allow the voice to be more open, vibrant, resonant, and clear.

- Check back in with your voice by trying your brief introductory paragraph again.

Is there a difference?

Reflective Journal

What did you learn about your body and the release work? What was different in the way you felt physically, emotionally, and mentally after the exercises? What questions came up for you as you worked? Which exercises worked best for you? What in your body feels different now than it did before? How would you describe how you feel right now? Was there a part of the exercise where you sensed a feeling of inner space? What has changed in your voice? Where in the body does the voice feel most alive?

_____

_____

_____

_____

(Continued)

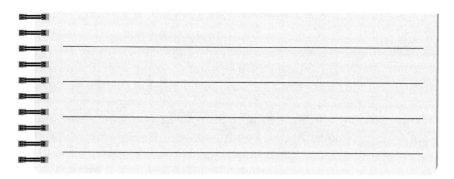

Aligning for Presence and Ease

In addition to the external barriers erected by society, women are hindered by barriers that exist within ourselves. We hold back in ways both large and small, by lacking in self-confidence, by not raising our hands, and by pulling back when we should lean in. We internalize the negative messages we got throughout our lives— the message that says it is wrong to be outspoken, aggressive, more powerful than men. . . . We lower our own expectations of what we can achieve.

—Sheryl Sandburg[12]

Familiar versus Natural Alignment

Two women attorneys are waiting in the same hall outside a court room. One is 5 feet 7 inches tall; her shoulders round down and her head and neck hang forward; her eyes are focused toward the floor. She sits with her arms folded and her legs crossed. The other woman is pacing the hall, walking heavily on her heels, her shoulders braced back, her elbows sharp, and her chin elevated. You are probably already forming assumptions about each of these women. They are both unaware that their bodies are communicating. Sometimes the messages we send out are not at all what we intend. People form opinions about us from the way we carry ourselves—the shape of the spine, whether it is long and straight or hunched and rounded, the position of the shoulders, or the lift of the chin. Our shoulders alone can speak volumes about our level of confidence, social effectiveness, health, and emotional maturity. People may even make assertions about personal discipline and intelligence based on how we carry ourselves— our alignment.

Our major body parts—head, neck, shoulders, rib cage, hips, knees, and feet—are naturally organized to counter the effects of gravity, to ensure that we move comfortably and breathe easily. In voice terms, natural alignment creates a foundation for the voice. Lifting the body into its natural state creates space for the diaphragm to move, space for breath in the lungs, and space for resonance in the throat and mouth. Natural alignment allows us to look confident, feel calmer, and sound clear and authentic.

Throughout our lives, beginning with our first steps onward, we have been forming habits of how we organize our bodies—how we stand, sit, and move. We are responding to feedback we receive from parents and peers. We are fulfilling our social and psychological needs. We are defending ourselves against the natural stresses of existence. In short, we are trying to survive. Thus, we develop our familiar alignment, which may not serve us vocally or physically.

Many of us are not aware that our familiar alignment, what we have grown accustomed to through years of habitual use, may be sabotaging our vocal potential. The head may jut forward, the shoulders round forward or press back, the rib cage caves in or thrusts out, or the hips push to one side. The feet may not be making solid contact with the floor. You probably recognize yourself in one or more of these images and want to answer, "But, Rena, this is just how I always stand; that's how I move naturally." It may be how you are accustomed to standing or moving, but it may not be the most efficient way for your body to function. If you want maximum vocal effectiveness, you need to look at your alignment.

Let's look at the components of *natural alignment*:

- There is the feeling that the body is moving up as it moves forward.
- The top of the head floats and lifts toward the sky as if helium balloons are tied to the base of the skull.
- The head sits easily on top of the spine, the face is forward, eyes are alert meeting the world.
- The chin is parallel to the floor.
- The shoulders are relaxed and down.
- The arms hang easily at the side.
- The pelvis is centered, neither tucked under nor pushed back.
- The knees are released (not locked).
- The feet are parallel, hip-width apart, with weight evenly distributed.

Understand that it is not only the voice that is linked to natural alignment, but physical and mental health as well.

If your familiar stance is caved, slouched, or rounded, your digestion can't work as efficiently; your back is compromised and will eventually lead to stiffness and pain, if it isn't already giving you problems. Also your physical state informs your emotional state. If we meet the world in a body that is not naturally aligned, we will likely feel a lack of self-confidence, with dark, heavy, or sad mood. We might even feel free-floating anxiety, when there is no reason to feel uneasy or irritable. Poor alignment affects our ability to take a deep breath, so we feel uneasy due to lack of oxygen.

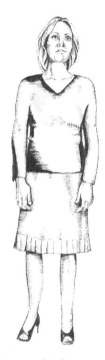

Poor Alignment   **Natural Alignment**

An adjustment in our alignment can lead to an adjustment in our sense of well-being. When our lungs are given space to fully inflate and our breath moves freely and deeply, the anxiety chemicals are cleared from the body. And of course, with a healthy breath comes a healthy voice. With natural alignment everything gets a little easier!

Video #3: Alignment into Presence
(Access the video at www.myvocalauthority.com/hervoiceinlaw. Enter the access code: HerVoiceinLaw1212.)

Exercise: Alignment

The following pages take you through natural alignment in detail. Some of these instructions are outlined previously, but more details are added here to build depth of learning and to change your internal focus. While working through these exercises, maintain a sense of ease as you go from your familiar alignment to your natural alignment. If you are working with an accountability partner, ask her to read the instructions while you physicalize the exercise. Then return the favor.

- **Feet:** Start with a grounded base, maintaining awareness of the feet in solid contact with the earth. Imagine that energy is drawn up through the soles of the feet; the whole of the earth is supporting the body as it speaks and moves.
- Place the feet parallel, hip-width apart.
- Shift your weight back and forth from one foot to the other several times. Rock forward and back from toes to heels. Find that place where the weight is evenly balanced over both feet. Imagine the bones in the feet spreading out across the floor.
- Imagine that the base of the big toe, the base of the little toe, and the heel form a solid triangle of support. Keeping the knees released, stand firmly on that base and relish the sense of strength it gives you.
- **Knees:** Release your knees with a gentle bounce. I call it "finding oingo-boingo" in your ankles and knees. Be aware of space and "cush" (a spongy feeling) in the joints.
- For the sake of contrast, lock your knees and try to breathe. With your knees still locked say, "Good morning, I am so pleased to be here today." Now release the knees, take a breath, and say, "Good morning, I am so pleased to be here today." It should be clear that the locked knees make deep breathing more difficult and that vocal ease, volume, and clarity are adversely affected.
- It is natural to lock the knees under the pressure of performance. It is part of the "fight or flight" mechanism that kicks in. A trained voice user knows to release, release, release, at the start of the presentation and at key points during it.

Release of the knees should not be confused with bent knees. A speaker does not have to go through life with permanently bent knees. It is a simple release as opposed to a lock. Go back and forth between locked and released to become more aware of the difference.

Pelvic Girdle and Tail Bone Awareness

The foundations of the torso are the pelvic girdle and tail bone. Common problems in this area have to do with the holding of muscles and habitual pelvic tilts, either too far forward or too far back. Each of these leads to breath problems and blockage of a fuller, richer, and louder voice. Ideally, a speaker wants to sound as if the whole torso—all the way to the pelvic floor—is involved in creating the voice.

The following exercises will increase your sensory awareness of the pelvic girdle and the tail bone. They will also help you find length in the lower spine and feel where the most efficient and released position exists for you.

- **Tail Bone:** Imagine that your tail bone has an eye on it and can actually see behind you, in front of you, or at the floor. Move the pelvic girdle so that the eye of the tail bone can see the wall in front of you. Push the pelvic girdle back so that the eye of the tail bone can see the wall behind you. Then allow the tail bone to look at the floor right underneath you. Repeat this exercise several times until you get a sense of where the tailbone is. Do this with ease.
- Shake the tail bone to release any tension and say out loud an easy "ahh."
- **Spine:** Imagine the base of the spine: think up the spine one vertebra at a time, easing and lifting all the way to the top of the head. It is as if your spine is growing from the top and the bottom. The tail bone is moving toward the earth; the head is moving toward the sky. The face is still forward; the eyes are now open to meet the world.
- Take a walk around the room, feeling the power in the spine. Your face is leading you forward, and the top of the head is leading you up. Be aware of the space between the vertebrae. Imagine you are taller. The feet are in firm contact with the floor; your arms are moving easily at your side.
- Stop and realign; think about the feet in solid contact with the floor, weight evenly distributed, knees released, length in the lower spine, the upper spine moving toward the sky, arms relaxed at your sides.
- **Shoulders:** Check to see that the shoulders are relaxed and down, the chest is wide, and the arms are hanging easily at your side.
- Bounce the shoulders several times up and down. Feel the weight as they come up toward the ear lobes; drop the weight heavily as they give in to gravity. Vocalize an "aah" as you jostle the shoulders up and down.

- Round the shoulders forward. Attempt to breathe and say the now familiar line "Good morning, I am so pleased to be here today." This is what you sound like in *denial*.
- Push the shoulders back; lift your chin. Again, attempt to breathe and say your line. This is what your voice sounds like in *bluff* mode. In either position, breathing and making sound were probably not easy.
- Bounce the shoulders up and down again and relax them in the down position. Feel the wideness of the chest. Breathe and say your line, "Good morning, I am so pleased to be here today." You should feel that breath is easier and sound is fuller.

Head

Think "long back of neck, soft front of neck, chin parallel to the floor." This is the position that creates the most space in the throat and back of the mouth. Many of us are chin-leaders. We press, stress, and emphasize with our chin. As soon as the chin comes up, we have closed off the space in the throat and the back of the mouth. The jaw and tongue become tense. The voice gets brittle, shrill, tight, or underprojected. From this position, the vocal folds have to do extra duty, which causes them to fatigue. As you explore the sensation of "long back of neck, soft front of neck," be aware that your jaw is released and that the tongue is resting on the floor of the mouth.

- Gently look right and left several times. Look down and up several times. Find a place of balance as the head rests on the top vertebra. The head is balanced when it won't drop backward or forward.
- Drop the chin to the chest and shake your head "no."
- Slowly let it lift back to neutral.
- Let your right ear drop gently toward your right shoulder and exhale on a "sh" sound. Let the head float back to neutral. Allow your left ear to drop gently toward the left shoulder, exhaling on a "sh" sound. Again, let the head float back to neutral. Do this slowly several times.

Putting It All Together

Natural alignment is an ideal: it is a starting point. A litigator may deviate from this as she gets involved in the heat of an opening or closing. But we start from and return to this place of natural alignment throughout a presentation or conversation, knowing this is the place of maximum inner space, support, ease, and efficiency.

Quick checklist:

- Feet are in solid contact with the floor.
- There is "oingo-boingo" in the ankles and knees.
- There is length in the lower spine as the tail bone lengthens toward the floor and the spine extends upward, floating toward the sky.
- The shoulders are relaxed and down, arms hanging easily at the sides.
- The head floats on top of the spine with long back of neck and soft front of neck.
- The chin is parallel to the floor.
- The jaw is relaxed, and the tongue is resting on the floor of the mouth.
- The breath is flowing easily.
- Take a walk around the room and enjoy the sensation of ease, energy, and lightness.
- Stop and realign. Try a bit of your introductory paragraph or count easily one through ten.
- Walk again briskly – not zombie-like, but alert and ready to do a job.
- Stop and try the speech again.
- For contrast's sake, try walking in your "familiar" alignment, your habitual walk, and say the same bit of speech as you walk.
- Now recover your "natural alignment," again creating space in the spine. Aware that breath is flowing in your body, walk briskly and say the speech. Go back and forth several times between familiar and natural alignment. Repeat your personal introductory statement. Be aware of the differences in the effort, quality, and volume of your sound.

Exercise: Forward Inclination and Natural Alignment

A simple and quick way to find natural alignment is through a forward inclination (spinal roll, introduced earlier).

- Stand with your feet hip-width apart, weight evenly distributed, long spine, released neck. Breathe slowly and deeply throughout this exercise.
- Let your chin drop to your chest. Slowly giving in to gravity, let the spine incline forward one vertebra at a time, until the head and neck are dangling free. The arms are released, the knees are bent, and you are breathing deeply. Sigh out as if the sound could just fall from the mouth.

- Start to rebuild the spine from your tail bone, stacking one vertebra on top of the other, like building blocks; the head is the last to come up. When the spine and shoulders are fully erect, lift the head, feeling the long back of the neck, the soft front of the neck, and a released jaw. Breathe into your center.

How does this feel? What does this do for your sense of alignment? Does the spine feel longer? What is happening with the lower spine? The pelvic girdle? The jaw?

Reflective Journal

Record what you experienced as you worked through the alignment exercises. What are your thoughts about your familiar alignment versus your natural alignment? At what point did you feel the greatest change or shift? Where in the body are you most aware of change? What is happening with the breath? Have your feelings or emotions shifted at all? How has your voice changed?

_____

_____

_____

_____

_____

_____

_____

_____

(Continued)

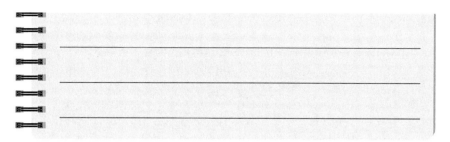

Breathing for Power

To breathe fully is to live fully, to manifest the full range and power of inborn potential. . . . it unleashes the energy of life providing pathways into the deepest recesses of our body.

—Dennis Lewis[13]

As human beings with our own emotional, psychic, and physiological history we have developed habitual patterns of behaviour that feel safe, right, natural, and real. If we try to alter these patterns of behavior, we may feel unsafe, wrong, unnatural, and false; particularly if we are in a situation of emotional stress, such as in training or rehearsal. Many of these behavioral patterns concern how we breathe—how we breathe for life, how we breathe to speak, how we breathe when we listen, how we breathe in different emotional states.

—David Carey[14]

I joined the children's choir at St. James Methodist Church in Tucson, Arizona, when I was in the third grade. I was just 7 years old, but I can still remember the first practice, where I sat, what I wore, and what songs we sang. Though only two other children showed up that Sunday night, I sang boldly, undaunted. It never occurred to me to wonder if I had talent—it didn't matter. I didn't feel exposed being one of only three—it didn't matter. I just did what came naturally to me—I sang! That was the beginning of a life-long love affair with all things voice.

I continued to sing in the church choir and the school chorus, took private voice lessons, studied acting, and performed in musicals. I even made a record that was briefly on the Top 40. All the while I was peripherally aware that breath was important. After all, every performance teacher I ever had told me so. But it wasn't until I was in London in 1999 studying voice at the Central School that I finally began to put it all together. David Carey, who provided the quote at the beginning of this section, was the course director. The underpinning of virtually every class he taught was breath—science, theory, and practice. His clear and thorough knowledge of the relationship between breath and voice led me to a deep appreciation of the power of deep central breathing, which has now become the centerpiece of what I teach.

Breath is the single most important factor in the efficient use of the voice. If the breath is not working, nothing else will work. Breath is the cornerstone of the free and released voice, and no amount of intelligence, talent, preparation, or sound systems can compensate for its absence. A responsive, flexible breath system translates directly to volume, quality, connection to authentic emotion, and ease of delivery.

Breathing is both the easiest and hardest task for a speaker to master. When I first introduce the concept of breath for speech, no matter the age group, I get a response something like this: "But Rena, I already know how to breathe. If I weren't breathing, I'd be dead." And I say, "Yes, but there are two types of breath: breath that sustains life, which you do involuntarily, and breath for speech, which we will learn takes a little more thought, practice, and attention."

Breath Is Voice!

What we hear and identify as human speech sounds is just disturbed air. We take in breath, and, as we exhale, the breath stream passes over the vocal folds, causing them to vibrate, disturbing the outgoing flow of air. So breath is the fuel that ignites the voice. The physical action of the movement of the breath is a natural and automatic response to the need to share the voice. It is a beautifully complex, integrated system that through focus and daily practice can become as easy as . . . well, breathing.

Breath Is the Master Key to Our Soul

The deep central breath connects us to who we are, to the core of the human being that lives inside us, to our most authentic self. Breath connects me to my intelligence, my creativity, and my spontaneous response mechanism. I learned this through years of training actors. An actor can learn her lines and movements and execute them perfectly; but if breath is not deep and central in the body, the audience will not be transfixed. The miracle of authentic communication cannot happen without it.

How Breath Works

In order to help us understand how the breath works, let's imagine that the voice is like a trumpet. For the trumpet to sound, you have to blow air into the mouthpiece. Breath is the power source. If you want the trumpet to be louder, you blow more air. It is the same with the human voice; if you want a louder, fuller sound, you need more air.

Indulge the voice geek in me here as we discuss the finer points of the deep central breath. As mentioned above, there are two kinds of breath: passive breath for sustaining life and active breath for speech. Breath to sustain life—both the inhale and exhale—happens unconsciously with minimal effort; the body instinctively does its job of keeping us alive. Breath for speech differs in that both the inhale and the exhale are conscious and take a certain amount of energy and muscular engagement. It takes a great deal of energy and breath to speak lengthy ideas, communicate weighty emotions, or fill a courtroom with sound.

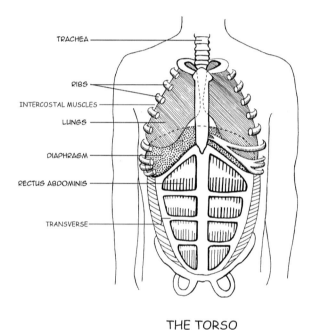

THE TORSO

The Breath System

The key anatomical players of the breath system are as follows.

1. The **torso** extends from the shoulders to the pelvic girdle, to the ribs on either side, and to the breastbone in front and the spine in back. This framework houses the lungs, stomach, and intestines.
2. The **diaphragm** is a large, dome-shaped muscle that bisects the torso, positioned under the lungs and on top of the stomach.
3. The **intercostal muscles** link the ribs and allow them to move up and out so that the lungs can fully inflate with air.

4. The muscles of the **abdominal wall,** specifically the **transverse,** are the muscles of breath support.
5. The **lungs** inflate with air on the inhale and deflate on the exhale.
6. The **vocal folds,** the sound source, are two flaps of tissue with a layer of muscle at the core that vibrate or oscillate when air blows past, creating tiny puffs of air, thus producing sound.

When breathing for speech, the brain sends a signal that it would like to say something; it has a thought that needs to be communicated with the voice. The body then prepares to inhale in readiness for speech. A release of the **abdominal wall** follows, the **diaphragm** contracts and drops, and the **ribs** swing up and out. This action of the diaphragm and the ribs creates a negative pressure in the lungs. Air rushes into the lungs to equalize this pressure.

When the lungs have sufficient air, the process reverses and the exhale begins. It is on the exhale portion of the breathing cycle that sound occurs; we speak on exhaled air. The diaphragm relaxes and begins a passive journey back up to its resting place. The ribs move down and in. The muscles of the abdomen, primarily the **transverse,** engage to manage the exhale in terms of duration and the amount of air that leaves the lungs. This muscular action of the transverse is what we refer to as "breath support." When a choral conductor says, "support your sound," or when your speech coach asks you to "use support," what they mean is to engage the lower abdominals so that you have adequate breath to support the voice for the length of the thought, phrase, or sentence.

The exhaled air flow travels up through the **windpipe,** where it meets the closed vocal folds. The air pressure builds up, causing the vocal folds to blow open and snap closed hundreds of times per second, releasing tiny puffs of air, thus producing sound. Imagine that the words are carried out on a stream of breath. Breath and sound are one. When the exhale stops, the sound stops.

How Breath Goes Wrong

When I was a young performer, I noticed that when I auditioned, my voice would become thin and lose power. I also found myself having to take breaths in places I had not before. I now know that the culprit was **high, shallow breathing**. When we are nervous or experiencing stage fright, chemical changes take place in the body. One of the first and strongest responses is the inability to take a deep breath. Under pressure, we instinctively resort to shallow breathing, which is not good for the voice and heightens performance anxiety. If your shoulders move up noticeably when you breathe in, you are filling only the top lobes of your lungs. That will not give you the breath capacity for a strong voice or the stamina to complete a complex thought without gasping for breath midsentence.

The majority of oxygen exchange happens deep in the bottom of the lungs. When we engage in high, shallow breathing, the oxygen never gets deep enough to nourish our brain, wake up our body, enliven our thoughts, trigger our creativity, or calm our nerves.

Another way that breath for speech can go wrong is through **weak abdominal release** on the inhale. When the abdomen releases, the diaphragm has more room to contract down, creating a larger space in the chest for more air to enter the lungs. Many voice users initially do what I call reverse breathing: they suck the stomach in on the inhale and push it out on the exhale. This leads to shallow breathing and a reduction in the ability to support the sound. Through the exercises that follow, we will learn how an easy abdominal release on the inhale is our touchstone. Remember, as the breath comes in, the abdomen releases and goes out. On the exhale, the abdomen, guided by the transverse abdominal muscle, moves toward the spine.

Another way that breath for speech can go wrong is through **lack of breath support** on the exhale, leading to insufficient air moving past the vocal folds. When the vocal folds do not receive a strong, steady stream of air for speech, they must work too hard, causing the voice to be pressed, strident, thin, and small, or lacking in range of emotion, volume, and quality. Lack of breath support can result in vocal fatigue at the least and permanent damage to the vocal folds at the worst.

We have already talked about **generalized tension in the body** and how it can sabotage the deep central breath. Locked knees, rigid pelvic girdle, tight stomach, restricted rib cage, and tension in the shoulders, jaw, or tongue all inhibit the system. This kind of tension is insidious because we are often unaware of its presence; it is so common that it feels normal to us. Locking the knees is an unconscious response to standing for a long period of time; couple that with any level of performance anxiety, and those knees want to lock up tight. The shoulders tend to creep up to our ears because of the tension we pick up throughout the day. Tension anywhere in the body creeps into other parts, setting off a chain reaction in the body. Localized or generalized body tension prevents the abdominal muscles from fully releasing, keeping the diaphragm higher and creating less space for the lungs, which are then forced to take in smaller amounts of air, causing the vocal folds to do double duty. You get the picture.

LAURIE

Initially, breath work was challenging—I was breathing backwards or some-thing. We worked on it a lot before I felt like I got it. When I started meditating, I picked up the breathing part quickly, thanks to the breath work Rena and I had done. You become aware that you have some control over when you breathe in and when you breathe out. Whether for speaking or meditating, that feeling of being grounded, centered, and calm is essential. I find that when I'm really anxious I am not breathing. I remind myself, "Oh yeah, breathe! Oh gee, that feels a lot better."

The following exercises for the breath fall into seven categories:

1. Connecting to the natural breath that sustains life
2. Releasing the abdominal wall
3. Sensing the moment of readiness
4. Engaging the transverse, which manages and supports the breath on the exhale
5. Building breath capacity and sustainability
6. Accessing support
7. Connecting breath to words

For some of these exercises you will need five or six sentences from an opening or closing, either one you are familiar with or one you are currently working on.

Connecting to the Natural Breath

For the following two exercises, you will need a drinking straw and a balloon.

Exercise: The Balanced Breath—Breathing Through a Straw

The purpose of the first exercise is to experience an easy, balanced breath while bringing attention to the natural movement of your center—the abdom-inal area. You are going to inhale and exhale fully through a drinking straw.

- Gently hold the straw in the middle and put it between your lips.
- Exhale through the straw on a slow four count. Then inhale through the straw on a slow four count.
- As you inhale and exhale slowly through the straw, put a hand on your belly so that you are aware of what is happening in your center. As you

exhale, your center will move toward the spine. As you inhale, the center will easily release out.

- Repeat these steps for several minutes.

If you have panic issues associated with breathing, the exercise *will not* trigger an anxiety attack. If you start to get dizzy, reduce the effort.

Exercise: Blow Up the Balloon

The purpose of this exercise is to give you a strong sense of what the center does when you are breathing for speech.

- Stretch the balloon so that it will blow up easier. Blow up the balloon at your own pace, taking in a new breath when you need to. Put a hand on your belly again and be aware of what is happening in your center.
- Be aware of movement of the transverse and of how automatic it is. The abdomen expands as you inhale—the deeper the breath, the larger the expansion. On the exhale, the transverse engages and moves toward the spine.

Under normal circumstances, we seldom need the amount of muscular engagement in the abdominals that you needed to blow up the balloon. Think of that as effort level ten. For normal speaking, one to one, in a deposition, you may only use effort level three or four. In court you may go as high as effort level eight. A truly responsive breathing system is easy and natural, happening without conscious thought on your part. That's why we train—to teach the body what it must do on its own—so that in the heat of summing up for the jury, we are free to concentrate on the real issues, like connecting with the jury and making your points clear.

 Video #4: Breathing for Power: Abdominal Release; Sensing the Moment of Readiness; Building Capacity; Breath Management; Accessing Support, Recoil Breath, Trampoline Breath & the Big Book; Connecting Breath to Words (Access the video at www.myvocalauthority.com/hervoiceinlaw. Enter the access code: HerVoiceinLaw1212.)

Exercise: Feeling Abdominal Release

Release of the abdominal wall is a challenging concept for a culture that worships the flat stomach. Many of us expend a lot of energy and effort to keep the stomach held in at all times. However, the speaker must learn to cast aside that ideal and embrace a belly that is relaxed, even (dare I say it) "poochie," on the inhale. On the inhale, the stomach area expands; on the exhale, the stomach moves toward the spine.

- Stand easily in natural alignment and be aware of how you are breathing. Stay with this for at least ten breaths. Don't try to change it, just be aware of your own breath rhythm. Where are you most aware of the breath entering and leaving the body?
- Place a hand just below your navel, and release the abdomen into your hand on each inhale.
- Blow all the air out of your lungs on a "fff" or "sh" and wait until your body needs a breath. When your body signals that a breath is needed, release the abdominal wall and feel a breath drop in. Repeat this sequence five times. Blow out all the air, wait for the need to breathe, and then allow a breath to drop in. You should feel the abdomen release and expand on each new inhale.
- Now let the natural breath rhythm just happen—the breath comes in, the breath goes out. Be aware of the pause that occurs after each cycle— breath comes in, breath goes out, pause. Repeat several times.
- Continue exploring the breath cycle—the breath comes in, the breath goes out, pause. Enjoy the pause, luxuriate in it, and wait gently for the need to start the cycle again. Notice that the quality of the pause determines the quality of the next inhale. Keep your knees soft, the back of the neck long, and the jaw hanging loosely.

Breathing in this way should feel natural and easy.

Exercise: Sensing the Moment of Readiness

You will want to revisit this exercise over and over to make it part of your daily warm-up. You can do this standing in natural alignment or sitting easily in a chair. Allow 5 minutes the first few times you do this, then 2 minutes when it becomes part of a daily warm-up.

- Find the natural rhythm of your breath: the breath comes in, the breath goes out. Notice the pause. When that rhythm is deeply established, turn your focus to the moment when the inhale becomes the exhale. Feel it deep in your torso. It may feel like a momentary suspension, an easy change of direction. Stay with this awareness for several breaths.
- Once you have established the awareness of the moment when the inhale turns to the exhale, mark that point with the word "now." Keep the knees soft, the back of the neck long, and the jaw released as you say "now" each time the inhale becomes the exhale. Repeat at least ten times. The word "now" reminds your body that it is ready to speak.

- Holding the awareness of the moment when the inhale becomes the exhale, lengthen the "now." Repeat several times, still focusing on the inhale becoming the exhale.
- Keep this focus and, with a big space in the mouth, let the sound lengthen to the full extent of the breath, saying "Now, even now, even now, even now." Repeat several times until you can feel that perfect moment of readiness: the point in the breath cycle when the inhale becomes the exhale and the body is ready for sound. Memorize what this feels like. Enjoy how easy it is to create full, rich, open sound with so little effort.
- With the knees still soft, the neck still easy and long, and the jaw still released, change to the phrase "Tomorrow and tomorrow and tomorrow." Feel it fly from your body; let the sound reach all the way across the room and touch the wall. Keep focusing on the moment when the inhale becomes the exhale. Repeat at least ten times.
- Change the spoken phrase to your introduction, "My name is . . . and I am. . . ." Repeat several times, still sensing the moment of readiness when the inhale becomes the exhale.
- Try four or five sentences from your opening statement. Breathe at thought changes, while maintaining the focus on the moment when the inhale becomes the exhale.

Exercise: Engaging the Transverse Muscle, Recoil Breath

- Say "sh-shhh" with enough power to expel all your air. Feel the recoil of the transverse muscle as it quickly and naturally releases to let the next breath come in. Repeat four times.
- Change the sound to "v-vvv" and repeat four times. Do the same with "z-zzz."

Exercise: Trampoline Breath

- Find your natural alignment, grounded and centered. Place a hand gently on your transverse muscle.
- Say "ha ha ha" quickly and lightly as if a little man is using your diaphragm as a trampoline. Repeat the "ha" until you need a breath, then let a breath fall in and repeat three times. Put a hand on your center so that you can feel the activation of the transverse muscle. Your effort level should be between three and four. Keep your jaw released and the tongue resting on the floor of the mouth.

- Say "hee hee hee" as if that same little man is jumping on the trampoline of your transverse. Repeat the sound until you need a breath, then let the breath fall in. Repeat three times.
- Say "ho ho ho" in the same manner as above.

At the end of this simple three-exercise sequence, you should feel that your transverse muscle has been engaged and enlivened. These exercises should be part of your standard daily vocal warm-up.

Exercise: Building Breath Capacity

The following exercises will help you in several ways. First, you gain a kinesthetic or physical understanding of the amount of breath needed for the size of the thought. A short thought requires a smaller breath. A larger thought, a bigger emotion, a longer sentence, or a larger space requires a bigger breath. You will develop the capacity to sustain an even flow of breath to match the length of the thought. In addition, you will increase the flexibility of the breath as you easily move from short to medium to long thoughts.

- Imagine that you are blowing out a single candle. Then imagine that you are blowing out ten candles. Finally, blow out 100 candles.
- Imagine you are holding a feather in your hand. Blow the feather off your hand. Keep the feather in the air with a stream of breath. Blow a handful of feathers across the room. Blow away all the feathers from a huge pillow that has burst open.
- Put your finger to your lips and gently "shush" a talkative movie patron seated a row in front of you. He does not get the message, so "shush" him louder. Then, "shush" him as if you would push him out the door with the force of your breath.

Notice, in each case, that you took the amount of breath necessary to fulfill the requirements of each escalating situation. As the circumstances became more urgent and the need larger, the amount of air taken in and the amount of force behind the released air also became larger.

Note: If you begin to feel a little lightheaded or dizzy while doing these exercises, take a break until it passes.

- Stand in natural alignment. Blow out all your air on a "shhhh," and when you need a breath, let one come in. Begin an exhale on "zz." Continue as long as you can comfortably sustain the sound. Don't go so long that you start to tighten or sputter. Renew the breath, and sustain the "zz" four to six times.

- You can also do this exercise on "ss." Try it both ways and see which sound is easier.

    By doing this kind of exercise every day you can double your capacity in a couple of weeks. This should also become a standard part of your vocal warm-up.

Exercise: Breath Management

This exercise helps your body learn the lessons of capacity from a short thought to a long thought. This time, the thoughts are going to take the form of numbers: one through ten.

- Find easy natural alignment. Knees are released, back of neck is long, and jaw is released. Say "one." Breathe. Say "one by two." Breathe. Say "one by two by three." Breathe. Continue on in this way to "ten." Be aware of what is happening in your center as you progress. Be aware of the ease of each new breath. The body knows how much breath it needs for the length of the thought coming next. This exercise should become a standard part of your vocal warm-up.

Exercise: Filling the Space

Doing breath work at home or in your coach's studio feels easy and safe. We think we have mastered it. Then when we move into the larger space like a courtroom, we suddenly go back to shallow breathing and pressing to achieve the volume required to fill the space. Use a sentence or two from your opening statement for the exercise below.

    When you transition from a small space to a large space, try this exercise:

- Raise the palm of your hand to about 16 inches from your face. Breathe that distance and speak several sentences to your hand.
- Extend your arm fully and breathe to the tips of your fingers. Speak the sentences to the end of your hand.
- Now look at the seats in the center of the room. Breathe that distance, make a little more space in your mouth, and speak to those seats, resisting the temptation to press from your upper chest or throat.
- Now focus on the wall furthest from you. Breathe that distance and speak your sentences. Resist the temptation to press from the vocal folds. Think more space in the mouth, keep the thoughts clear on your lips, and release your knees. If you fill the body with breath and open your mouth, you will be able to fill the space with sound without pressing or shouting![15]

I have a few tips about dealing with dizziness or lightheadedness, which happens frequently when doing breath work.

- Keep the knees released.
- Reduce the effort.
- Open your eyes and focus on the palm of your hand.
- Take a break from the exercise for a few moments.

Exercise: Accessing Support by Pressing against a Wall

Accessing Support

Support was defined earlier in this chapter as the abdominal muscles, primarily the transverse, engaging to manage the flow of the exhale as we speak. If you want more vocal power, volume, or gravitas, you need to dial up the energy or engagement of the abdominals. If you have a long sentence or a large emotional thought, you engage your abdominals for an extra boost. When we are first made aware of the importance of support, but we have never done it, we may need a quick and easy kinesthetic nudge as to what that is and how it feels.

- Stand facing a wall. Place both hands on the wall, slightly below shoulder height. Lunge forward with your dominant foot to give you a stronger base. Press your hands against the wall at a moderate energy level, enough so that you feel the abdominals engage, but not so much that you feel tension in your throat. Breathe in, then speak, counting one through ten or your introduction. Feel the engagement around your middle powering your sound. Keep your throat open so that it feels like a megaphone for the power in your center. When we want more power or volume, our natural tendency is to press from the throat. Imagine that your power control is in your center and that your abs are doing all the work. As you press into the wall and explore support, keep the back of your neck long and the front of your neck soft. Don't let tension radiate to your vocal folds.

- Now step away from the wall and try your voice again. Try to maintain the sense of engagement you felt in your center as you pressed against the wall.

Exercise: Connecting Breath to Words

- Print a hard copy of an opening/closing. Read it out loud, breathing at each major punctuation. Take your time and find the moment of readiness at each new breath. Your body memorizes where the breath goes, just as your brain memorizes the words.

Reflective Journal

Reflect on the straw, the balloon, abdominal release, and sensing the moment of readiness. What did you learn about the breath that you did not know before? What did you learn about capacity, sustainability, and breath management? Which exercises gave you the easiest and most natural sense of the breath as it moved in and out of the body? What is the moment of readiness like for you? Describe in your own words how it feels. How does this awareness affect the voice? How does the moment of readiness affect your understanding of how the breath works to support the voice? What insights did you have? What questions came up? What sensations did you experience? What did the speech feel like as you breathed at each punctuation?

_____

_____

_____

(Continued)

Opening the Megaphone

The research is overwhelming. Not only does the sound of your voice matter twice as much as what you're talking about . . . but voice in lower frequency range will encourage others to see you as successful, sociable, and smart . . . a high-pitched voice, particularly for women, is a career-stunting attribute . . . shrill voices have the hint of hysteria that drives men into a panic. . . . A woman with a high-pitched tone will be perceived as not only unleaderlike but out of control.

—Sylvia Ann Hewlett[16]

My Mouth Is My Megaphone

We all know the voice Ms. Hewlett is talking about in the quote above—fingernails on a chalk board. The *perceived* pitch of a woman's voice has as much to do with resonance as it does with the *actual* highness or lowness of pitch. Resonance is maximized very simply by making space in the mouth. Your mouth is your megaphone. If you want more sound, open your mouth. If you want more vocal warmth, open your mouth. If you want to sound more leader-like, open your mouth. If you want to sound more accessible, open your mouth. It is that easy, but it can be challenging, particularly if your lifelong habit is to speak through a very small space.

To understand this concept, let's dig a little deeper into what resonance actually is. How do you know the difference between the sound of a violin, a cello, or a stand-up bass? What is it about the quality of the sound that identifies each instrument? How would you describe a trumpet's sound in contrast to a tuba? A trumpet is bright; a tuba is full and rich. Just as each musical instrument has a distinctive quality, each human voice has attributes that are unique and have an emotional effect on the listener.

Can you describe the difference between the voice of James Earl Jones and Fran Drescher of *The Nanny* fame? Soothing, mellow, comforting for Jones, as opposed to piercing and brittle perhaps for Fran. Or Gwyneth Paltrow and Roseanne Barr? Gwyneth's sound is warm, mellow, or smoky, while Roseanne might be bright, nasal, and abrasive. Which voice would you rather listen to? Most listeners respond positively to Jones and Paltrow, negatively to Drescher and Barr, even as we admire and laugh at their comedic abilities.

We use the word **quality** to describe that distinctive, individual sound. A component of vocal quality is **resonance,** the process by which sound created at the vocal folds is amplified, enriched, and filtered in the resonating chambers of the body. In a very general way, I think of resonance as disturbed air (breath that has been set in motion by the vocal folds) bouncing around the hollows of the body gaining energy, amplifying some qualities, and dampening others. These body hollows make up the **vocal tract**: the throat, the mouth, and the nasal cavity. Resonance is your body's natural amplifier.

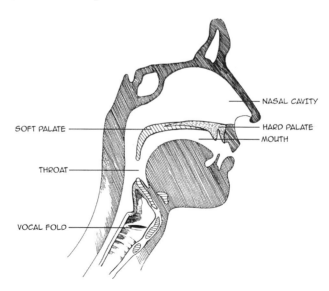

Vocal Tract

The trombone has a larger, lower tone than the trumpet. Why? The trombone has a bigger resonating tube. In turn, the tuba will always have a bigger, deeper sound than the trombone because it has the biggest resonating tube. The human voice has a resonating tube as well—the throat, mouth, and nasal cavities. We have an advantage over brass instruments in that ours is flexible, and it can be made longer, shorter, wider, or thinner. If you lengthen your neck, you have changed the shape of your vocal tract. If you extend your lips forward, you have changed the shape of your vocal tract. If you smile broadly or close your mouth tightly, you have changed the shape of the vocal tract and will change the quality of your sound. I maintain that it is more about a woman's resonance than her pitch that makes a voice pleasing or not. Pitch is discussed in more detail in the next section.

Taking the brass instrument metaphor a step further, what happens when you put a mute in the end of the trumpet? The sound is muffled. The human voice has natural, built-in mutes—the jaw, tongue, and soft palate—that can likewise muffle our sound, dampening resonance and making quality less compelling. If our mutes are filled with tension, they can suffocate the quality of our sounds. If they are open and relaxed, our voices will be warmer and more inspiring. Our task then, as speakers, is to make sure our resonators are open and free of tension. In this section, we focus on three parts of the vocal tract: the **jaw**, the **tongue,** and the **soft palate**, all of which can house hidden tensions that dampen and restrict resonance.

The **jaw**, in voice terms, is a large hinge that serves as a gatekeeper to aid in suppressing and controlling strong emotions. The masseter, the muscle that opens and closes the jaw, is one of the strongest muscles in the body. The effort expended to keep the jaw rigid results in tension, which backs up into the throat and stifles the resonance. To maximize space in the throat, we need to relax the jaw. It is not about creating a big space at the front of the mouth; it is about releasing the jaw at its hinges, creating space and length between the back molars. The jaw should naturally drop straight down as it opens and releases to gravity. Keep in mind that tendons link the jaw to the throat and finally to the larynx itself. Tension in the jaw radiates to tension in the vocal folds. If the jaw remains held or tight, the vocal folds will also tighten and constrict, causing them to work harder, leading to loss of power, ease, and clarity.

The **tongue** is a huge muscle that often has a mind of its own. We are aware of the front or tip of the tongue because we can see it, but the real culprit is the back or root of the tongue. It can carry tension that we are not even aware of, pulling back and down into the throat, muting our sound, and dampening clarity and warmth.

The **soft palate**, which lies at the back edge of the hard palate (roof of the mouth), has limited mobility, but what it has can be maximized. A flat soft palate can dampen sound and give the voice a nasal quality by allowing air to escape down the nasal cavity. We want a lifted palate, which creates a big space in the back of the mouth and maximizes the oral resonance needed for speaking in large spaces.

I frequently speak of resonance in terms of vibration. Laurie likes the word "buzzy." When resonance is activated, we feel vibrations buzzing in the throat, jaw, face, chest, and sometimes even the top of the head. As speakers, we want to maximize vibrations and to open our bodies up to them.

LAURIE

My neck, jaw, and tongue is where my stress goes. When my chiropractor or massage therapist is working on my neck and jaw, they invariably comment about how tight I am, "Geez lady, relax." I didn't realize that tension also affected my speech. I overarticulate, trying too hard to make it clear. I have early childhood memories of having difficulties with certain words, W's and R's, and being told by my parents to be clearer. Then forensics reinforced that. In debate, I was told to spit my words out. "Here, put marbles in your mouth and clearly speak around them." In retrospect, that was kind of a dangerous, stupid thing. When I am relaxed and do the warm-ups, I speak with less effort. I notice when I get tired I fall back into those old habits. It's still something that I have to work on regularly. And it starts with jaw, tongue, and soft palate.

 Video #5: Jaw and Tongue; Soft Palate; Humming, T'ai Chi, Archer; Kazoo (Access the video at www.myvocalauthority.com/hervoiceinlaw. Enter the access code: HerVoiceinLaw1212.)

Exercises: Jaw Release

The following set of exercises promotes the opening of the vocal tract and the releasing of vibrations, thus maximizing the resonance of the voice.

- Clench the jaw. With your fingers, find the place where you feel the knot or tightness and rub that spot. Now release the clench and let the jaw hang as you continue to massage at the jaw hinge.
- To further release the jaw, use the heel of your hand to massage the jaw hinge in downward motions. The focus is on releasing the jaw to gravity,

not forcing it open. With each pass of the hand, the jaw releases a bit
more. Repeat five times at a slow rate of speed, and remember to breathe.

- Take hold of your chin with both of your hands—with thumbs underneath,
  forefingers on top—and open and close the jaw with your hands. Imagine
  that the jaw is passive and that the hands are doing the work. Remember to
  keep breathing and maintaining a sense of length in the back of the neck.
- You might want to sanitize your hands before doing this exercise and
  have a tissue ready as it can be juicy. Cross your hands at the wrist. Put
  your thumbs inside your mouth and press them against the jaw hinge—
  that hard spot between your upper and lower molars. Press straight
  back into that spot. Sustain a medium amount of pressure for at least
  5 seconds. When you release, open and close the jaw to see if an easier
  space has opened up. This is acupressure for the jaw.
- Relish the feeling of a loose jaw, released and hanging. Lips can be open
  or gently closed as long as you maintain a feeling of space.

Exercise: Tongue Release

- While the jaw is hanging loosely, having given into gravity, shift your
  focus to the tongue. Be aware that the tongue is resting on the floor of the
  mouth, with the tip gently touching the bottom teeth.
- Allow the tongue to fall out of the mouth past the lips. Feel it lengthen gently toward the floor. Then stretch it gently toward the ceiling. With tongue
  still hanging out, send it first toward your right ear, then toward your left.
  Allow the tongue to gently clean the lips as if you have just taken a bite
  from a big juicy peach and you don't want to miss a drop. Clean the
  inside of your mouth with your tongue.

Exercise: Tongue-Speak

This is a silly exercise, but it has a profound and immediate effect. Try it
just once and I know you will be a convert. I use it as part of my everyday
vocal warm-up and again right before I present (clearly not in front of an
audience—that's what bathroom stalls are for).

- Let the tongue hang out of your mouth, and count out loud from one to
  ten, keeping the back of the neck long. Relax the tongue back into the
  mouth, letting it rest on the floor where it normally does. Count out loud
  again with a sense of a released jaw and tongue.
- Say a few lines of your opening in tongue-speak, allowing the tongue
  to hang loosely out of the mouth. Then speak the same passage with the
  tongue easily back in the mouth.

Be aware of the ease that is created when the tongue and jaw take their rightful places as relaxed articulators and not as tension spots forcing you to artificially create a louder sound.

Exercise: Soft Palate

- Yawn widely with the tongue gently against the bottom teeth. Enjoy the yawn—stretch with the arms as if you have just awakened from a restful night's sleep. Be aware of a huge space opening at the back of the throat. Do this several times to remind the throat that being open and released allows for optimal resonance.
- Sound the consonant "ng," as in the word "sing." To make this sound, the tongue and soft palate come together. Feel the point of contact. Release the "ng" into an "ah" and feel the tongue and palate move away from each other. Repeat the following sequence slowly: ng-gee, ng-gay, ng-gah, ng-go, ng-goo. Feel the tongue and palate coming together on the "ng" and flying apart when you open to the vowel sound.
- Imagine that you have a big, juicy peach in your hand. Lift it to your mouth and prepare to sink your teeth into it as if to take a large delicious bite. Feel the lift of the soft palate. Repeat and just before your teeth are ready to sink in say, "Hello," or perhaps, "Tomorrow and tomorrow and tomorrow." Repeat the bite of the peach each time you refresh the breath, creating a large, easy, open space. At the moment of readiness say, "Why fly so high," or "Four score and seven years ago," or "Ask not what your country can do for you, ask what you can do for your country." You can also use lines from your introductory paragraph or opening. On each new breath, lift the imaginary peach as if to bite.

Through these two exercises, you are building an awareness of the lifted soft palate. You are also teaching the soft palate, through muscle memory, the raised position for confident speech that carries forth effortlessly.

Exercise: Humming to Increase Vibrations

- Humming is one of the easiest ways to release vibrations and increase resonance. Start a comfortably low hum with a big space in the back of the mouth. Hum until you feel the need for a breath, then breathe and start the hum again. Tap gently on the chest to loosen the vibrations. Feel that you can fill your upper chest with vibrations. Keep the back of the neck long and the space in the back of the mouth wide.

- Raise the pitch a little and continue to hum with a long back of the neck and a big space between your back molars. Move the hum around on your face or chew so that the facial muscles are moving the hum around. Explore various pitches in the lower to middle part of the voice as you continue to hum.
- Blow through the lips on a hum (think of horse lips). Let the pitch vary in small loops as you blow, widening the loops of pitch as you continue to hum. This gathers and increases the strength of vibrations and begins to loosen the pitch range.
- To bring vibrations forward say: key, key, key, key, key. Speak this on a middle pitch, keeping the back of your neck long. Aim these vibrations on the back of the upper teeth.
- Intoning is singing on one note comfortably in the middle of your range. In this exercise you are going to intone the phrase "My mother makes marmalade." Find a pitch in the middle of your range and sing the phrase on the same note, really enjoying the "m" sounds. Then *speak* it in the same place where you felt the intoning. Even if you think you can't sing, I encourage you to play with this anyway—you have a beautiful voice!
- Next, intone these phrases: "My mom makes more money than most men." "Many more moms making much more money." After you intone, speak the phrase in the same place you felt the energy of intoning.
- Finally, try the first paragraph of your opening and intone it. Breathe at the end of each thought until you have intoned the entire paragraph. Feel the vibrations forward in your mouth. Then say your speech with attention to the spot where you felt the most vibrations while intoning.

Exercise: T'ai Chi Sequence

For some attorneys, the following two exercises are out of the comfort zone. But try them anyway. They are extremely effective for building a resonant, strong, and flexible voice.

This exercise is based on a T'ai Chi sequence. It contains three basic movements accompanied by a sound progression. The goal is to connect vibrations to breath, waking up the voice easily and fully. This warm-up can be done toward the beginning or at the end of each session in order to bring all parts of the voice on line.

- Stand in natural alignment with the hands easily in front of the thighs. Throughout the exercise, keep shoulders down, neck long, and knees soft.
- On the inhale, bring hands to shoulder height. On the exhale, push the hands back down as you make sound according to the sound sequence below.

- Again, on the inhale, bring hands to shoulder height again. On the exhale, extend arms straight out and then down as you sound.
- Next, on the inhale, bring hands all the way up and over the head. On the exhale, open arms out and down as you sound.
- The sound sequence starts with humming. All three movements—up and down, up and out, and up and over—are made on a hum. Open the next sequence to an "ah." Then, change to "oo," followed by "eee." Finally, advance to any vowel, any pitch.
- A fun variation is "Ninja T'ai Chi" which is any vowel, any pitch, and any movement. While sounding, you can move any way you want, using arms in extravagant circles, arches, and loops. On each inhale, the hands come back to their original starting position.

Exercise: The Archer

This exercise warms up vibrations and encourages the whole body to open to resonance. It can be done as part of a larger warm-up. As this exercise also focuses the mind and calms performance anxiety, "The Archer" is an ideal single warm-up, if time for a full warm-up is not available.

Archer

- Widen your base so that feet are further apart, approximately 24 inches. Bend the knees a little, keeping the back straight and the neck long. Cup the left hand easily at the waist; the right arm is across the body with the hand flexed, palm out.
- While exhaling on a hum, the right arm moves to the right across the body, until it is straight to the side. On the inhale, the right hand cups at the waist, and the left arm crosses the body.
- While exhaling on a hum, the left arm moves across the body, until it is straight to the side. This movement sequence repeats, sounding the hum four or five times. The sound opens to an "ah," then "oo," then "ee," and finally any vowel, any pitch, repeating the physical sequence five times on each sound.

Exercise: Kazoo for Forward Resonance

Forward resonance carries the voice out into space, making it easier to project to the back of most rooms. Many of us let our resonance fall backward, down into the throat. The purpose of this exercise is to feel forward resonance and to practice it in a way that will help us carry the sound in a professional speaking situation. Some women's voices can sound nasal, a quality that is unpleasant to our ears. Another female habit that is increasingly being used is **vocal fry**, which is the falling off of the voice toward the end of sentences, letting the pitch drop to the bottom of the voice. It is heard on television sit-coms and in popular movies; some stereotypically recognize it as a "sorority girl voice." The vocal fry habit sends many young women to speech therapists when they start losing their voices. It also gives away a young woman's vocal power and authority.

You will need an inexpensive kazoo. (I buy them in bulk from the local party supply store.)

- Put the big end of the kazoo in your mouth and hum. You will feel vibrations around the mouth. Hum a tune just for fun; your school fight song is always a good choice. Now with the kazoo in your mouth, speak/hum a portion of your opening into the kazoo. Take the kazoo away, and speak the speech in the same place you felt the vibrations from the kazoo.
- Do the whole speech, one sentence at a time, first with the kazoo and then without, speaking in the same place where you felt the energy from the kazoo.

I once had a very talented student who had a terrible case of vocal fry, a habit that she had tried to break for several years. I had her put the kazoo on a string around her neck for an entire semester. Whenever she spoke in vocal fry, either socially or on the stage, I said, "Kazoo it!"

She would say the sentence into the kazoo and *voila*, she was back on voice. If you have any kind of resonance issue, either too far back, in the throat, in the nose, or vocal fry, make the kazoo a part of your personal warm-up every day. It is a quick reminder to your body where healthy, clear, forward resonance should live.

Exercise: Resonating Energy Centers

This final resonance exercise is for those of you who want to make meditation part of your daily practice and build the voice as well. It is an excellent warm-up for full body resonance as well as for deepening the breath and extending the pitch range. It also has a calming and focusing effect.

The purpose of this exercise is to center the breath, encourage vocal vibrations, and open the body's receptivity to vocal resonance. This exercise can be done daily or several times a week. It generally takes 10 minutes to engage with it fully.

- Sit in an easily erect position, eyes closed, with a long back of the neck, jaw released, and focus on your breath.
- Focus on your tail bone and intone the vowel "eh" on a comfortably low pitch, imagining that you can send vibrations to that area. Repeat each sound to the end of the breath at least five times.
- Focus your attention on the space just below the navel; the sound is "oh" (as in the word "go"), and the pitch is slightly higher. As you sound, imagine that the "oh" sends vibrations into and spinning out of the abdominal area. Strengthen the vibrations and feel that space come to life from the energy of the sound vibrations. Repeat each sound to the end of the breath at least five times.
- Next, your focus moves to the area between the navel and the sternum. The sound is "ow" (as in the word "out"), and pitch again moves naturally up a tone. Feel vibrations of sound move to and spin out of this area. Repeat each sound to the end of the breath at least five times.
- Now focus on your chest; the sound is "ah." Feel vibrations move through the chest, lungs, and heart. Feel that area come alive with your sound vibrations. Repeat each sound to the end of the breath at least five times.
- Shift the focus to the throat and mouth area; the sound is "oo" (as in goose). Feel the area come alive with vibrations as the sound spins through it. Adjust pitch up to maximize vibrations in the throat and mouth. Repeat each sound to the end of the breath at least five times.
- Move the focus to the forehead; the sound is a hum. Adjust your pitch up so that you feel vibrations in the forehead. Imagine that the vibrations are streaming out of the forehead. Repeat each sound to the end of the breath at least five times.

- Now focus on the final energy center at the top of the head; the sound "ee" (as in eat) helps to move vibrations into that area. Let the pitch move up as well. Feel the sound vibrations spin out of the top of the head; imagine a long stream reaching all the way to the sky. Repeat each sound to the end of the breath at least five times.
- Now let your voice glide easily up and down from the tailbone through the top of the head and back, using any of the above sounds. Just let the voice play. Be extravagant as you let the sound motor throughout your pitch range.
- Slowly find your way to standing and to natural alignment. Try a few sentences of your introduction or part of an opening to see if your body is more receptive to the vibrations of the voice, the pitch is freer, the sound more released, and the breath more deeply rooted in your body.

Reflective Journal

Take a few moments to reflect on resonance. What did you learn that you had not thought about before? What did you discover about resonance and your voice?

Which of the exercises was most useful? What have you learned about space in the mouth? What do you plan to take on as part of your personal voice practice?

_____

_____

_____

_____

_____

_____

_____

_____

_____

_____

_____

Sidebar

I am repeatedly struck by how women (including myself) undercut themselves through their way of speaking. Upon reflection, trying to identify a woman whose speaking style I look up to is, in many ways, as frustrating as trying to identify female role models. A woman I frequently communicate with has adopted a strange style of droning on and on and on, laying out the question very carefully, but also implicitly sending the message that our time is not valuable. It drives me crazy. Another woman comes to mind who has an almost incomprehensible speaking style, full of "ums" and "ehs" and breathy, almost airheaded circumlocutions. That is also incredibly frustrating/ counterproductive and actually sort of passive-aggressive. In the absence of a role model, I am finding my own path to presence and clarity through a daily Buddhist practice that has allowed me to hear and notice my true self through chanting. I continue to try to apply this insight to my speaking voice, but I remain both frustrated and amused by how difficult that continues to be.

—Ellen McClure, Professor, Administrator

Articulating for Ease and Clarity

Language holds power. When it's filled with confidence and passion, and backed up by authentic presence, it can transform us. . . . Declarations create and clarify vision for ourselves and others. . . . It doesn't matter where you are on the path to leadership . . . declarations make leaders. . . . People who boldly put themselves out there are more interesting, memorable, and charismatic. They exude presence. We admire their pluck and daring. We orient ourselves differently around them.

—Kristi Hedges[17]

The words you choose and how you say them are a crucial part of owning your authentic voice. Think of the most dynamic attorneys you know. They use language vigorously; and we respond! Each word is carefully chosen and fully articulated. Dynamic language has muscularity and space. By muscularity I mean the lips, teeth, tongue, and soft palate come together and move apart with energy and specificity. By space I mean space in the mouth; remember the megaphone image in the last section.

It might be helpful here to look at why clarity and energy of language are such challenges for presenters, speakers, and leaders. The casual nature of contemporary culture leads us to casual speech. With casual speech comes a mouth that doesn't want to open; thus, vowels are not given ample space, and consonants are weak to the point of nonexistence. If we are using "contemporary casual speak," the articulators—lips, teeth, tongue, and palate—don't want to come together in an energized way; they approach each other but don't actually make contact. If our habit is to use language in casual or sloppy ways, it will feel very foreign, self-conscious, and even awkward to use the articulators with more energy. But if your goal is to win over a jury, probe for the truth, sign a new client, or impress the partners, you must use your articulators in a more athletic way. The exercises below will help you push back your comfort zone and develop new and more effective ways of using language in your "professional speak."

Energetic, dynamic speech starts with articulation. By articulation we mean that the clear formation of vowels and consonants as the articulatory surfaces of the lips, teeth, tongue, palate, and soft palate come together and move apart within the space inside the mouth. In this section, we will practice:

- Articulation of vowels and consonants
- Flexible, responsive articulators
- Clarity of thought

Western spoken languages are made up of two major sound categories: **consonants** and **vowels**. In the General American dialect alone, there are twenty-three consonants and nineteen vowels and diphthongs. These sounds are literally made all over the mouth, and the mouth needs to work harder for professional speech than it typically does for social interactions. Through awareness and practice, these sounds become more specific, clearer, and more emotionally engaging.

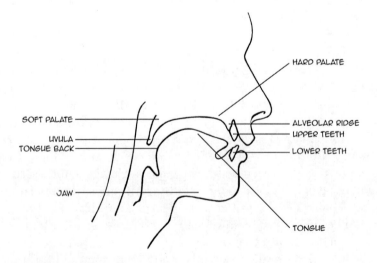

Chart of Speech Organs

In the illustration of the speech organs, you will notice the articulators, which include the lips, teeth, tongue, palate, and soft palate. Each of these organs needs to be exercised and sensitized to the specificity required for clear speech.

 Video #6: Articulation: Consonants; Vowels; Spacer, Mouthing, Every Part of Every Word
(Access the video at www.myvocalauthority.com/hervoiceinlaw. Enter the access code: HerVoiceinLaw1212.)

Consonants

What are consonants? Everything that is not a vowel! Right, but consonants are much more than that. A **consonant** is defined as an obstruction of air flow. Back to the breath: when you speak, air is flowing, and the vocal folds are vibrating against each other, creating tiny puffs of

Looking at mouth in hand mirror

disturbed air. That stream of air is obstructed in some way by the articulators, and we have created a sound we know as a consonant.

Exercise: Explore Articulators

Using a small hand mirror, look at your mouth:

- Look at your **lips**. Bring them together, making a popping noise as they come apart. Say **p b t d k g**. Try these sounds several times, energetically bringing the lips together and feeling them fly apart with the force of the breath. Look at your lips in the mirror as you do this.
- Try **f v s z sh ch**. Try these sounds several times, energetically bringing the lips and teeth together feeling the energy of the air hissing through.

Exercise: Flexibility

To build strength and flexibility, repeat the following sounds several times, feeling the energy of each sound. Be sure to breathe!

- puu tee kaa, puu tee kaa, puu tee kaa, puu tee kaa
- buh dah geh dah, buh dah geh dah, buh dah geh dah, buh dah geh dah

Exercise: Consonant Drills

Repeat the following phrases several times at a three- or four-volume level (too much volume on consonant drills can cause unwanted tension). Remember to check in with natural alignment, deep breath, and space in the mouth. Enjoy the full energy of the consonants, particularly final consonants. Really wrap your mouth around them, using more muscularity than you normally would. Don't rush or overproject.

- Unique New York, unique New York, you know you need unique New York.
- Big black bugs brought buckets of Black Beard's blood.
- Red leather, yellow leather.
- My mother makes marmalade to make Marv merry.
- Let us go together to gather lettuce.
- Five frantic fat frogs fled from fifty fierce fishes.
- Cheryl's cheap chip shop sells cheap chips.
- If a hair net could net hair,
  How much hair could that hair net,
  If a hair net could net hair?

Exercise: Mouthing

Going back to the opening/closing speech you have been working with, "mouth" the entire speech; that is, really use the articulators, but create no sound. Fully engage the lips, teeth, tongue, and palate, as if you want a person across the room to read your lips and you dare not utter a sound. When you have completed mouthing the entire speech, speak the text on voice, paying as much attention to the articulators as you did when you mouthed.

Exercise: Every Part of Every Word

With the same speech, at volume level two, slowly pronounce every part of every word, every tiny syllable, every middle and final consonant. When you have finished the entire speech, speak at a normal pace and volume level.

Vowels

I chose to start our speech discussion with consonants, but of course that is only half of the picture. Vowels are the other branch of clear and expressive speech. If consonants are the bones of speech, then vowels are the heart and soul. Some say that while consonants carry the clarity of meaning, vowels impart the emotional content. I have observed that both vowels and consonants must be fully realized for speech to be clear to the ear and piercing to the heart.

Vowels are created by unobstructed air flowing through an open mouth. We change vowels by changing the shape of the mouth.

Exercise: Long Vowels

Let's look first at long vowels. These are vowels that sustain for a period of time.

ee as in <u>ea</u>t
ah as in f<u>a</u>ther
oo as in g<u>oo</u>se

- Try the long vowels, repeating each several times with energy. Explore pitch, levels, and length as you fully experience each vowel before moving on to the next.

   ee as in <u>ea</u>t
   ah as in f<u>a</u>ther
   oo as in g<u>oo</u>se

Exercise: Short Vowels

In contrast to the long vowels, we also have short vowels that are quicker in duration.

> *i* as in k<u>i</u>t
> *eh* as in <u>e</u>very
> *uh* as in str<u>u</u>t
> *u* as in p<u>u</u>t

- After you have said the vowel within the context of the sample words above, isolate each short vowel and feel its quick, incisive energy.

Exercise: Diphthongs

Diphthongs are two vowels that are spoken as one sound. There are five in the General American dialect. As you speak the following words, pay close attention to the underlined diphthongs, feeling the blending of the two vowels to form one.

> *ay* as in f<u>a</u>ce
> *i* as in pr<u>i</u>ce
> *oy* as in ch<u>oi</u>ce
> *o* as in g<u>oa</u>t
> *au* as in m<u>ou</u>th

- Explore the diphthongs, repeating each several times with energy. Explore pitch, levels, and length as you fully experience each vowel before moving on to the next.

Exercise: Vowels Only

- Using your opening/closing speech, speak only the vowels and diphthongs, eliminating all consonants. Do this easily, letting the vowels flow one into the other, avoiding choppy glottal attacks (when vocal folds smack together with excessive effort). Don't worry about getting each one perfectly in order; speak the essence of the vowels, using a kind of "soupy," free-form modern dance rendition. I find it helpful to move with this exercise, so everything is kept free and open. The focus is on carving out the space in the mouth for the vowels.
- When you have completed the speech in vowels only, find natural alignment, let the breath settle, and speak the entire speech. Be aware of what has happened to the vowels as a result of the exercise.

Exercise: Clarity of Thought

After the consonants and vowels have been worked and your articulators are warmed and energized, the next step is to make each thought clear.

- Say your speech as if you are thinking each word as it comes out of your mouth. You chose each word for a reason. You need to fully breathe, make space in the mouth, and enjoy each word.
- Give yourself the strong intention to be clear enough so that a listener can take notes on what you are saying.
- Finally, speak it freely, release it, and trust that the work you have done on muscularity and specificity will be there. You don't have to think about it. Your body just does its job while you focus on the effect you are having on the listeners.

Exercise: Record Your Speech

Thanks to the convenience of smart phones, you can easily watch and listen to yourself work. Record the speech you are working on. I know you can overcome being self-conscious about this and learn to watch and listen to yourself objectively. Which words are not clear? Are you falling off at the ends of sentences? Are you using fillers "uh," "um," "like," "ok?" They are easier to banish when you actually hear them yourself. Are your final consonants clear? Are you giving vowels space and shape?

Always warm up your articulators before any presentation, whether speaking to one person or to a group. Use any of the exercises above or create your own, but it is mandatory that you make articulation a part of your daily warm-up.

Dialects

An important word here about dialect. English is the language of business in this country and in many places throughout the world. General American is the dialect of English spoken in the United States by some professionals. But this does not imply that General American is more proper or standard while other dialects are somehow improper and substandard.

If you speak English with a dialect, whether regional within the United States or international, I encourage you to speak it proudly. It reflects where you have come from and who you are. I don't feel that everyone needs to have perfect General American; how boring would that be! Dialect bias, however, is real. From time to time, jurors or even clients may expect and want to hear a nonregionally specific dialect, trusting only someone who sounds familiar. If you have been given feedback that you can't be understood or if you simply want to learn a General American dialect to use when the situation calls for it, a dialect coach can help. Check out the Voice and Speech Trainers Association website, Professional Index, https://www.vasta.org/professionalindex/alphabetized, for coaches in your area.

Lisps

I have noticed an increase in issues associated with the *s* consonant among speakers. It is a sound that varies widely from speaker to speaker. It includes the whistling *s*, slushy *s*, lisps, and tongue thrusts. To oversimplify, it is caused by excess tension in the tongue tip as the *s* is formed or by the tongue coming too far forward. To effect a change in this usage habit requires daily practice, often under the guidance of a speech therapist. I have found a CD that is very helpful, distributed by Voice Print Publishing, called "The *S* Drill" created by Ginny Kopf, www.voiceandspeechtraining.com. An s issue is a speech habit that can limit professional opportunities. It can be lessened or eliminated with consistent daily practice.

Sidebar

I am first generation from Mexico. English is my second language and that has been an issue from a very young age. When I get nervous, I get self-conscious about whether or not I'm pronouncing words correctly. I start to slow down. Because the minute you have an accent that people don't recognize, you've just added another thing to overcome, right? In the courtroom. To a jury. It is always an issue for me and I'm self-conscious about it. But I am learning that being comfortable with yourself means accepting your culture. I am proudly a product of my culture. I can be both reserved and quiet but also fiery and feisty, that is cultural with me and it has served me well as my career has progressed.

—Stephanie Duran, Attorney

I don't know any woman who hears her own voice and thinks it's great. When I first heard a recording of my voice I was devastated. But at the end of the day, this very voice, I'm convinced, made me a success here in Oklahoma. My dialect was so Tennessee it made make me stand out. People didn't always remember my name but they did my voice.

—Gale Allison, Attorney

Reflective Journal

Now that you have learned about consonants and vowels, how they are defined, and how they are formed, describe how your understanding and awareness of the specificity of sound have deepened. How did it feel to use more muscularity in your own speech? What exercises were the most effective for you? What will you take on as part of your personal practice?

_____

_____

_____

_____

_____

_____

_____

_____

Caring for Your Voice

Many professional voice users—including teachers, clergy, and politicians—do not give much thought to the manner in which they speak, much less take precautions to prolong the life of their voices and to prevent potentially career-ending vocal injuries. Once hoarseness, throat pain, or vocal fatigue occurs, individuals suddenly become acutely aware of the integral role voice quality plays in communication and find themselves scrambling to learn behaviors and techniques to rehabilitate their voices.

—Kate DeVore and Starr Cookman[18]

A Little Anatomy Lesson

Now that you are better acquainted with your voice through the work we have done so far, you are ready to explore more deeply the science behind how it works and the process for taking care of it. As we dedicate time and study to using the voice in more commanding and dynamic ways, it might help to have a better understanding of how the voice actually works. If we are truly changing from the inside out, picturing what is happening inside can be very powerful. I find it helpful to imagine how the various parts work together.

For most voice users, including many attorneys, the voice is a mystery. Sometimes it works; sometimes it doesn't. Sometimes the sound is all there and it feels great; sometimes it sounds hoarse, husky, thin, shaky, beyond our conscious control. What I want to do in this section is remove the veil of mystery from the voice. It can be understood, taken care of, and used in such a way that it is predictable and reliable. The voice should serve you, and not the other way around.

In my work I speak a lot about the vocal folds. What are they? Where are they? How do they work? How do I know when I am hurting them? After I cheer at a football game, I have no voice at all—what's that about? All these questions can be answered with a little understanding of how the major parts work together.

- **Breath:** The power source—breath is the fuel that makes the voice sound.
- **Vocal Folds:** The sound source—two flaps of tissue with a layer of muscle at the core in the larynx. They open and close against the air stream, creating the sound we call voice.
- **Resonators:** The amplifier source—the throat, the mouth, and the nasal cavities, which serve as your megaphone to make sound louder. This is also called the vocal tract.
- **Larynx:** The voice box, housing and protecting the vocal folds. The Adam's apple is the most visible part of the larynx.
- **Diaphragm:** A large dome-shaped muscle that sits under the lungs and on top of the stomach; it bisects the entire torso. It contracts and moves down on the inhale, allowing the lungs to fill with air.

How We Make Sound

Let's take a brief, deeper dive into how these structures work together to create voice sound. First, the brain sends a signal that it wishes to speak. The abdominal muscles release and the diaphragm contracts and moves down, creating negative pressure in the torso, which causes air to rush into the lungs. When air pressure in the lungs is sufficient, the diaphragm relaxes and moves back up, and the abdominal muscles (specifically the transverse) engage to manage the outgoing air flow. In the singing world, this is known as "support." Air rushes past the vocal folds, causing them to open and close hundreds of times per second, creating tiny puffs of air. These puffs of disturbed air move to the resonating chambers of the throat, mouth, and nasal cavities, where they are amplified and enriched. Your mouth is your megaphone! The articulators then turn this sound into intelligible speech. What an amazing process!

Vocal Hygiene

You only get one voice in your life. If it breaks, you can't go out and buy a new one. So you must know how to care for it to insure that it lasts a lifetime. You need to learn to protect those two delicate vocal folds, which I have said are about the size of your thumbnail. Make no mistake: keeping your voice healthy is under your control, and it is your responsibility. How your voice feels and functions is not a matter of chance or genetics; it is a matter of conscious choice and daily attention. If you make large demands on your voice, you should be aware of what the voice needs to stay healthy.

If your voice gets fatigued when you speak, if you finish the day with a hoarse or husky voice, or if your volume is weak, review the good vocal usage habits you have learned in the previous sections.

- Release habitual tension before you speak.
- Practice natural alignment, grounding, and centering.
- Breathe deeply and centrally when you speak.
- Make space in the mouth.
- Speak at optimum pitch.

In addition to vocal usage habits, a few life-style adjustments can make a difference.

Get Plenty of Rest

Boy, this is a hard one. The voice is one of the first places in the body to feel fatigue and the last place to feel rested. We live in a society that remains sleep-deprived much of the time. We expect our bodies to perform at high levels, often with insufficient rest. However, if you want your voice to be in the best possible shape, the body and the voice need to be well rested.

In addition to rest at night, your voice needs periods of quiet throughout the day, particularly if you are a heavy voice user. I talk to my clients in terms of "vocal units." This is a metaphor for thinking about the endurance capacity that a voice has throughout any given day. For example, let's say that you have ten vocal units available to you each day. You may use three units in the morning as you shout at your child to get ready for school. You may use three more vocal units as you greet a colleague in a noisy office. Three or four vocal units may be spent cheering at your daughter's soccer game. Then if you have a presentation to make, you only have one unit left for a task that may require four. If you must use your voice beyond its daily unit allotment, the voice will begin to show fatigue. It may not be as loud, it may sound a bit husky, or you may feel a thickness in the larynx. A little quiet time with a cup of warm tea can provide a welcome rest for your voice.

Budgeting vocal units is a very important aspect of maintaining good vocal health. If you know that the greatest demands on your voice will be made at a 3:00 presentation, proposal, or closing, then you should start conserving vocal units for the period of highest need. Each person's vocal units are different. Some people have voices of steel, with a seemingly endless supply of vocal units. These fortunate few are able to use, and even abuse, the voice for long periods of time without any negative effects. Others may fatigue after a lengthy conversation on the phone. You can increase your vocal units with proper usage, thinking length in the back of the neck and using adequate breath support. But the concept that your voice can give you just so much in a day must be honored if you want to keep the voice healthy.

Drink Plenty of Water
Water keeps the vocal folds hydrated, which is very important in maintaining general vocal health. Fifty to eighty ounces of water a day is a good estimate, depending on your size. My clients get used to carrying a bottle of water with them all the time. Be especially diligent about hydration both before and after a demanding presentation. A good rule of thumb: you know you are well hydrated if you "pee pale."

Avoid Caffeine, Carbonated Beverages, Acidic Juices, Milk, and Alcohol
This warning is particularly true before heavy voice usage. Caffeine and alcohol are diuretics, draining moisture from the body and more specifically from the vocal folds. Milk can cause an increase in phlegm, which can lead to the need to clear the throat. For my part, it feels that carbonated beverages strip natural moisture from the throat and create gas in the stomach, which can surprise a speaker in embarrassing ways. Acidic juices can irritate the stomach, which can cause reflux that irritates the vocal folds. Not all people react to these beverages in the same way. You need to know your voice and give it what it needs to operate at optimal efficiency. When in doubt, drink room temperature water or warm herbal tea.

Avoid Talking in Competition with Loud Noises: In Subway Stations, Airplanes, Noisy Parties, or Near Loud Music
Talking over noise causes our vocal folds to work harder. We do it unconsciously. My recommendation is to avoid using the voice in these situations if possible. When it is not possible, be sure that you are using deep central

Poor alignment while talking on the phone

Healthy alignment while talking on the phone

breathing and keeping a long back of the neck. Social chitchat and talking on the phone can be great vocal unit drainers as well. Think about the alignment you assume when talking on the phone; most of us literally let the body cave in on itself; effort goes right to the vocal folds and stays there.

Don't Smoke

I don't know that I even need to mention this warning; most people are aware of the dangers of smoking, and more people don't smoke than do. We all know cigarette smoking causes all kinds of health issues, including heart disease, stroke, cancer, high blood pressure, and premature aging of the skin. Cigarettes also have a profoundly negative effect on the voice. Smoking is like cooking the vocal folds. They stay constantly inflamed and are more susceptible to hemorrhage, infection, and swelling. Over time, the smoker's voice gets huskier and hoarse, and pitch range diminishes as the vocal folds lose elasticity. Secondhand smoke is equally hard on the voice.

Avoid Screaming

Athletic events and shouting at friends over loud music are two situations where screaming is common. With adequate breath support, length in the back of the neck, and space in the mouth, you should be able to project the voice at a level that allows you to enjoy the game or to be heard by your friends without suffering total laryngitis the next day.

Avoid Pushing Forward with the Head and Neck While Speaking

It is common for us to extend the head and neck as we speak, particularly if we are intent on making a point. This postural habit, however, shortens the space in the back of the neck, raises the tension level in the jaw and tongue, and cuts off the ability to access deep breathing. In both social and professional settings, I can improve my voice usage immediately by keeping length in the back of my neck and breathing a little more consciously and deeply.

Be Aware of Certain Medications

The antihistamines that you might need to take for allergies can be drying. Be sure to drink more water while taking these medications. Avoid throat sprays that numb pain as they can make vocal folds more susceptible to strain, infection, or irritation. Since mentholated lozenges are drying to the vocal folds, find nonmentholated substitutes.

Take Care of Acid Reflux

Acid reflux (heartburn or indigestion) can bubble up and irritate the vocal folds, causing you to sound hoarse or husky. If you have regular bouts of heartburn, or if you feel a constant need to clear your throat, try Maalox or Mylanta and avoid eating heavy, fatty, or spicy foods before bedtime. If it is a serious problem for you, a doctor can prescribe an acid blocker like Nexium.

Add a "Cool Down"

After a full day of speaking, it is helpful to "cool down" the voice, just as a runner walks around and stretches before she stops. Try a couple of these fatigue-soothing exercises: easy humming in the middle of the range, gently humming into your kazoo, or slowly breathing in and out through a straw. Yawn, stretch, and sigh out gently on an "ah"; repeat several times.

If you earn a living by using your voice, I encourage you to follow these guidelines so that you can avoid the "scramble to rehabilitate," as described in the quotation that opened this section. Precaution is the key!

Now that you have learned and practiced the foundational elements of voice and tuned your instrument, in the next chapter we will focus on enhancing your presentation skills to catch their interest and capture their hearts.

Chapter 2
Catching Their Interest

Phrasing, inflection and pitch are what distinguish you as a person worth listening to. . . . As in music, it is important to deliver your words conscious of your narrative arc, lifting and dropping your cadence to emphasize key passages or points, paying attention to how you end a phrase . . . so your listeners sense closure and they consequently hang on to the last word and retain it before making room for the next thought. The uplift that younger speakers impose on the ends of their sentences . . . undermines the whole message by denying this closure.

—Sylvia Ann Hewlett[19]

What is it that holds the jury's attention? What makes a juror remember details? What makes a juror believe you and then be brave enough to go into the jury deliberation room and advocate for you and your client? What draws a potential client to believe in you as her advocate? What is it that compels a witness to reveal facts to you?

As we answer these questions, I want to take you back to your image of the litigator from heaven. When I tried to think of iconic images of excellent attorney delivery, the first which comes to my mind is Gregory Peck as Atticus Finch (the obvious choice, right) or Matthew McConaughey in *A Time to Kill*, both compelling for very different reasons. But I want to talk about women attorneys, role models who give us examples we can study, discuss, and learn from. There are actually a number of films with women attorneys in featured roles, including *Beyond a Reasonable Doubt, Guilt by Association, Jagged Edge, I Am Sam, Plain Truth, Word of Honor*, and *On the Basis of Sex*. Among the twelve most famous lawyers of all time, according to Google, only three women are listed: Hillary Clinton, Gloria Allred, and—wait for it—Judge Judy. Among celebrated women attorneys on YouTube, I found video clips of Michelle Obama, Lisa Bloom, Kyrsten Sinema, Barbara Jordan, Janet Napolitano, Kathleen Sullivan, Caroline Kennedy, and forty or so more. As I watched and listened to each (and I encourage you to do the same, with your growing awareness of compelling delivery techniques), I was struck by how much vocal variety I encountered. How often in each of them does something in the voice change? Notice shifts in rate from slow to fast, in pitch from high to low, in volume from loud to soft, and shifts in quality or tone from comforting to interrogating, inspiring to punishing. Each time a change of any kind, subtle or broad, happens, audiences sit up and pay more attention. If two sentences in a row are the same, the audience checks out, stops listening, and starts to focus instead on their internal chatter, which is way more interesting to them than you are.

LAURIE

Starting in high school as a debater, I was told a man has a deeper voice and a deeper voice is better at projecting through the whole courtroom, so they are going to own that arena. Which translates to me as, "I have to make my voice lower," even though I'm 5'2" and not really designed for that. As far back as high school forensics there were comments about voice and body language that were gender based—cross your legs when you sit at a table; you are strident. They were molding us into the societal expectation of what it is to be female, taking away options for vocal variety and flexibility. After working with Rena, I am much more aware of pacing, pitch variation, and projection levels. I still struggle with dropping words at the ends of sentences. But at least I know I am supposed to carry my energy forward. Each time I work on it, I get a little better at it, so it feels more natural and authentic at this point.

Expanding Pitch Range

In front of the whole class, a professor in law school told me that I had the most irritating voice he'd ever heard—totally embarrassing! I was not aware that there was anything wrong with my voice, nor had I received any feedback to that effect. I started working on not having such a high-pitched voice. I have come to believe that a woman does not have to raise her voice to be heard.

What she has to say is more important than being the loudest in the room. Obviously good speakers, female speakers, who are better able to tell a story, are more successful.

—Esther Sanders, Attorney

As I said earlier, the pitch of a woman's voice is perhaps her most talked about vocal attribute. We hear feedback such as, "Her voice is shrill, high, thin, or small; her voice grates, or she sounds like a little girl." Expanding pitch range is the goal of many top-notch speakers and is relatively easy to do, given regular practice.

We may better understand the concept of **pitch** in musical terms as in a note that can be high or low. Although the speaking voice does not sustain pitch the same way as in sung music, pitch is always present. **Pitch range** is the distance from the highest note to the lowest note that an individual voice can use—it is a range of pitches that a speaker has at her disposal. Most of us use only a few notes of pitch variety in our professional speech and even fewer in our everyday speech. The developed voice can have up to eight or ten notes of usable pitch range. This is not to say we should use all ten within every utterance, but use of more dynamic highs and lows in pitch range makes us more compelling to listen to.

Anatomically, pitch is the result of tension, or amount of stretch, in the vocal folds themselves. The more stretched and thinned the folds, the higher the sound; the more relaxed and bunched the folds, the lower the sound. Think of the strings on a guitar: the fatter, looser strings create lower notes, while the thinner, tighter strings generate higher notes.

We only have to think of the monotone law professor, whose lecture drones on with no pitch variety, to know that one-note communication puts us to sleep. The speaker who uses her full voice and pitch range to express her enthusiasm and knowledge of her subject engages and holds us. Now that you have a working knowledge of pitch, listen online to any speech by Michelle Obama. What do you notice about pitch range and variety? The more you listen to her and others, the more easily you will recognize it in yourself. Through the exercises in this section, you will become comfortable using more pitch variety yourself.

In our contemporary relaxed culture, a pitch issue for women, particularly younger women, millennials, is to sit on the bottom of the range, to speak in our lowest notes. Young women want to be taken seriously or sound sexy or, like Laurie, were told that lower voices have more authority. So they use their lowest notes, in a vocal style we call **vocal fry** because it trails off into a frying-like sound. Tune into reality TV shows that feature young women and you will hear this quality. Vocal Fry is an authority thief, a gravitas stealer.

There are, by contrast, some young women who keep their little girl voices long after they have physically grown beyond that. Sometimes for psychological reasons, they are hanging on to past behaviors and relationship patterns that feel comfortable. Or the thin, high-pitch sound has become so habitual that they don't try other vocal behaviors. Continuously speaking in either extreme of the pitch range is not effective for the professional female's speaking voice because it limits expressive options, hampers the ability to be heard and understood in larger spaces, and can lead to vocal health issues where loss of voice can become a real possibility.

Another power-stealing vocal trait is known as **up-speak**, the raising of pitch at the end of declamatory sentences, turning statements into questions. It makes a woman sound as if she is unsure and seeking approval. Up-speak is discouraged in legal settings because it weakens both the message and the speaker. Felicia Collins Correia, a nonprofit executive, had this to say about up-speak, "Young women today have this question mark at the end of what they say . . . don't think they recognize how invalidating it is, how undermining. It is not cute, not strong. It doesn't give you the credibility you are seeking."[20] An exercise in the following section addresses up-speak.

Inflection is the pitch movement over the entire sentence, helping you to make your message clear. I sometimes call it the "tune" of the sentence—where words go up in pitch, where they go down. To understand why this is important to the expressive attorney, it helps to know that an audience (jury, client, witness) gets information in two ways: from the meaning of the individual words themselves and from the inflection of the sentence. If you speak a sentence or phrase without appropriate inflection or in a monotone, the listener only gets half of the information. For example, when a speaker is using antithesis or contrasting ideas, items, or actions, which we do frequently in legal settings, the listener needs to hear a large pitch change from one idea or action to the next in order to recognize that a contrast is being made. The inflection communicates the meaning.

Rampant in our culture is **falling inflection**, which is the dropping off of pitch, volume, and energy at the ends of sentences. We all do it, and it weakens our message, making us sound uncertain and failing to inspire buy-in. There is an exercise below that will help you identify this habit and put a new one in its place.

Video #7: Pitch Range: Ng Siren; High/Low; Pitch Absurd, Master Thespian; Pringles Tube for Optimum Pitch, One to Ten Shoot for the Middle
(Access the video at www.myvocalauthority.com/hervoiceinlaw.
Enter the access code: HerVoiceinLaw1212.)

The following exercises will expand your pitch range, release more varied inflection, and help you avoid both up-speak and falling inflection disease. They are fun and quick, and they add zest to a warm-up. Do these in the middle of your warm-up, after the voice has been motoring comfortably. Work at a moderate effort level, and stay loose and easy.

Exercises: Expanding Pitch Range

Ng Siren

- On the "ng" sound, make a tiny baby or puppy whine; repeat easily several times.
- Stay on "ng" as you begin to siren in ever-expanding loops of pitch— high-ish to low-ish (not highest to lowest), easing your voice into higher and lower places.
- Change to an "eee" siren, again in loops of pitch that go from high-ish to low-ish notes. Remember: soft knees, long back of neck, soft front of neck and breathe.
- Change to an "ooh" sound, letting your pitches swoop and glide. You might, at this point, want to add movement: as the pitch goes up, the body goes up, and as the pitch goes down, the body goes down.
- Expand to any vowel and any pitch. Be extravagant as you explore swoops and glides, and let your body follow. There is no right or wrong; just enjoy the pitch and body moving together.

High/Low for Expanding Pitch Range and Expressivity

Below are two lists of contrasting words. The first word in each pair inspires a higher note. The second word feels as if it needs to be spoken on a lower note. Physicalize, letting the body go up as pitch goes up and down as pitch goes down. Have fun—and do this with flair!

High	Low
Light	Dark
Sweet	Sour

Happy	Sad
Success	Failure
Laughter	Tears
Friend	Foe
Love	Hate
Joy	Sorrow
Generous	Miserly
Tickled	Tormented
Freezing	Melting
Healthy	Sickly
Rich	Poor
Reward	Punish
Win	Lose

After you finish the entire list above, read the opening/closing you have been working on, letting the inflection go where it wants to go. You should hear some new inflections which feel authentic and natural. No one wants to hear you deliberately striving for pitch and inflection variety. It should sound natural and easy, not calling attention to itself.

Say the above list again, reversing or mixing up the words in the right and left columns, so that you are not always going from high to low. This time truly infuse each word with meaning as well as changing pitch. Go immediately back to your own speech. Is your authentic inflection getting clearer and easier?

Exercise: Pitch Absurd

- Speak your opening/closing statement and let the pitch move up and down extravagantly, randomly, using pitch extremes, regardless of content or meaning. If moving physically a bit helps you and your voice stay released, then move as well.
- When you have delivered the whole speech in Pitch Absurd, find natural alignment, release your knees, keep your back of neck long, breathe, and just say the words, letting the pitch go where it naturally wants to go.

Optimum Pitch

Optimum pitch is the note around which our voice is the clearest, easiest, most efficient, and resonant. Learning to use optimum pitch in professional speaking situations is one of the best things you can do for vocal expressivity, authenticity, health, and efficiency.

Many of my clients are startled when they discover that their optimum pitch is higher than they think it should be. They don't want to sound like little girls. I then demonstrate the power of resonance. I can speak at my optimum pitch *without* full resonance and indeed sound like a little girl. When I engage the full complement of resonators (releasing jaw and back of tongue, lifting the soft palate) at the same pitch previously used, then I sound like a woman with a clear, easy voice. As Laurie told us, the prevailing sentiment is that a lower voice is more trustworthy and commanding. However, speaking below optimum pitch stifles expressivity and vocal variety. It traps the voice and makes it sound pressed and strident. Many women attempt a lower voice by lowering the larynx, which is hard on the vocal folds. Speaking at optimum pitch with free and open resonators will give you more vocal options and will be less taxing.

LAURIE

My natural pitch is a lot higher than I was speaking. We are taught that a woman needs to have a low voice to command the courtroom. Working with Rena gave me the freedom to get away from "lower is better." Speaking in my natural pitch range gives me more flexibility and resonance. It is challenging to overcome forty years of habit, but I love that "buzzy" sound of optimum pitch. The Pringles tube exercise reinforces that. It's a lot more fun to talk when it's buzzy. I didn't even know what resonance was. I had the intellectual understanding of it but no physical understanding of it until this exercise.

What follows are four ways to find your optimum pitch and strategies to help you integrate optimum pitch into your professional voice.

Exercises: For Optimum Pitch

Pringles Tube (for this exercise you will need an empty Pringles tube—happy homework as you eat the contents)

- Hold the empty Pringles tube (without the lid) gently between your thumb and fingers and bring it close to your mouth, not quite touching your lips. Vocalize into the tube on an "ah." Starting at your lowest comfortable note, going slowly up, one note at a time. Give the sound a moderate energy and volume level. Four or five notes up you will feel a vibrational change in the tube. When you reach your optimum pitch, the tube will vibrate in your hand, and you will sound noticeably louder. This is not magic—the tube is a biofeedback tool that amplifies your optimum pitch; it feeds back to you your most resonant sound.
- Once you find your optimum pitch, speak your full name on that pitch: "My name is . . . and this is my optimum pitch." If you lose it, go back to the tube and find it again. Once you can speak your name at that pitch, try a few sentences of your opening/closing. Go back to the tube as often as you need to.
- Find your optimum pitch and speak your entire speech. Be aware of how it sounds and feels.

Exercise: One to Ten Shoot for the Middle

If the Pringles tube did not work for you, this next exercise may help.

- Count out loud, one to ten, speaking the odd numbers high-ish in your range, the even numbers low-ish in your range. Keep the back of your neck long and front of your neck soft, and don't lead with your chin. Once you have counted to ten, without thinking, planning, or judging, shoot for the middle note and say "My name is . . . and this is my optimum pitch." Then speak a few lines of your opening/closing. It should sound and feel similar to the results from the previous exercise.[21]

Exercise: Five from the Bottom

- Find your lowest comfortable note, vocalize on "ah," and move up five notes. That should be your optimum pitch. Say "My name is . . . and this is my optimum pitch." Try a few lines of a speech.

Exercise: Uh-Huh

- A quick way to access optimum pitch, is to find your authentic "uh huh," the second note of which is usually your optimum pitch. I sometimes use this exercise when I am doing voiceover work and I feel my pitch is sitting on the bottom of my voice. I need to bring the voice back to its "sweet spot" quickly. I speak an "uh huh," and the second note of that is my optimum pitch!

A final word about optimum pitch. Although we call it optimum pitch, it does not mean this is the only pitch at which to speak. Think if it as your "center note," with pitches above and below. It is the note around which you will find ease of natural inflection that communicates meaning.

Curing Falling Inflections

Falling off at the ends of sentences is a serious problem for many speakers. It is a habit that can be quickly cured with a couple of simple techniques. These exercises let you naturally feel the lift and the forward moving energy from thought to thought. Do these exercises as many times as it takes until your body learns this lesson. Again, use your opening/closing speech.

Exercises: For Falling Inflections—Point the Final Word

As you say the last word of each sentence, strongly point with your index finger, fully extending your arm. Do this for the entire speech. When you are done, go back to the top and try your speech again and see if your body remembers how to lift the end of sentences in an authentic way without the finger point.

Exercise: Toss the Ball

Hold a tennis ball in your hand. On the last word of each sentence, toss the ball up (*on* the word, not after).

Exercise: Kick the Box

Put an empty cardboard box on the floor in front of you. *On* the last word of each sentence, kick the box. Kick with a moderate effort level, so that you are not bashing the box against the wall. Be aware of what the action of kicking does to the last word of each thought.

Exercise: Master Thespian

Another range-extending exercise is Master Thespian which, like Pitch Absurd, encourages the speaker to be extravagant vocally and physically. It is inspired by an old *Saturday Night Live* skit in which Jon Lovitz and John Lithgow dressed as ambitious, egomaniacal Shakespearean actors, overacting outrageously, voicing and physicalizing in a broad, stereotypical way, mocking the acting styles of that period.

- Using your opening/closing, try out Master Thespian, with my permission to totally overact. Use extravagant physicality, pitch range, and vocal qualities. When you have finished the entire speech, find natural alignment, ground, center, breathe, and say the speech again, allowing it to be whatever it is, as influenced by the previous exploration.

Reflective Journal

Describe how your pitch range reacted to these exercises. What changes did you notice? What places in your range seemed to be more comfortable and flow more easily? Did any parts feel creaky or unnatural? Consider the work you did with pitch range, optimum pitch, Pitch Absurd, and Master Thespian. What discoveries did you make about your habitual use of pitch and pitch range? How is your optimum pitch different from your habitual pitch? How does it feel? Where, specifically, do you feel the changes in your voice? How can you integrate this new knowledge into your daily practice?

(Continued)

Varying Rate

Rate variety is a powerful expressivity tool. It keeps the audience on their toes, drawn in to you, wondering what is coming next. Some voice and presentation trainers make distinctions among rate, pace, tempo, and rhythm. For the sake of simplicity, I just use the term *rate*. Rate is how fast or how slow you speak.

Most of us have a default rate that we use most of the time—it can be fast or it can be slow. More people speak too quickly; not nearly as many speak too slowly. I have, however, coached attorneys where my primary feedback back was, "Now say that again, only this time twice as fast." Our characteristic speaking rate is part habit and part lack of awareness. However, I find that most people race because they are not breathing deeply enough. The subconscious is afraid it will run out of breath, "so I better speak as quickly as I can before I run out of air." If, as you practice your speeches out loud, you breathe at each punctuation, you should notice that your rate is more deliberate and the words are more expressive and clear.

In our work on developing rate variety, there are three speeds—slow, moderate, and fast. By trying out each deliberately, we will begin to know when to slow down and when to speed up. When we have a lot of explanatory or stage-setting information, we can go pretty quickly. When we have points that the jury must remember, we slow down and get very deliberate and clear. The audience is most attentive at the point at which the change in rate occurs.

Exercise: Rate Variety

Using your opening/closing, speak it through as quickly as you can clearly say the words.

Read it again as slowly as you can clearly deliver it—not exaggerated like a movie in slow motion, but at a pace where everything is an important point.

Read it a third time at what feels to you like a medium or moderate rate.

Try the speech one more time, with some sentences fast, some medium, and some slow. These are random choices, just to get changing rate in your body.

By this point, you may be finding specific sentences that need to be spoken faster and some that need to be very slow. Mark in the margins **F** for fast, **M** for moderate, and **S** for slow. Now try the speech one more time, following your prompts.

If you are not sure how this actually works, see the example below. Speak it out loud, varying your rate. **M** is moderate, **S** is for slow, and **F** is fast (but not faster than you can clearly deliver the words).

Example:

M	Now let us turn our attention to the most important reason we are here. And that is to
S	assess the damage to Tony Overton.
M	Let me give you a preview of what that evidence will be. And make no mistake about it,
S	the damages that we speak of are permanent, deep, and will last every minute of Tony's life.
F	As you can see from the time this happened on January 30, 2015, it has already been more than three years since this fall.
S	And for that entire time the defendants have denied that they are responsible.

Once you have tried this example, go back to your own speech and deliberately explore rate variety. Your first choice may not be the right one. You may have to try each thought at several different rates until it feels right.

Using the Pause

*The ability to be comfortable with a pause is central to gravitas.
It says that you trust yourself; that you are not desperate to please
or to fill a silence. In a moment of silence you understand the truth
of the old acting rule that the most powerful person in the room has
the most relaxed breathing pattern.*

—Caroline Goyder[22]

Many people are uncomfortable with silence. They often babble to fill the silence, or they may use filler words or nonverbal sounds. Many teachers (I am guilty of this myself) ask a question and then rush to answer it themselves rather than wait in silence for a reluctant student to offer an answer.

But silence or a pause can be a very effective tool. You can intentionally build in pauses for dramatic effect. A pause is appropriate after you deliver the zinger, a statement or word that is crucial for the jury to hear. Let the phrase or the word hang in the air a bit before you go on to the next thought. If you are setting up important information or a "gotcha moment," you can insert a small pause before the zinger. The pause after information should be no longer than a three count, whereas the pause before information should be a one count.

And breathe. A pause for the speaker to hold her breath is distancing. Keep breathing deeply—it will make you more comfortable through the pause; you won't feel compelled to speak through your own silent dramatic moment.

Sidebar

I have a background in theatre. So I'm quite comfortable with projecting and being heard. But I have found that silence is effective. If someone interrupts me while I am speaking I will stand silently and stare at the judge. The judge sees this and will frequently stop that person, saying, "Yes, Ms. Pence, do you have a response?" I generally say, "Yes, Your Honor, I do."

I also find that standing in silence is effective if the other side is bringing up a number of points I have not been able to respond to in argument. I will stand up at my table, which tells the judge I would like to respond to this. The other side sees you stand and is distracted, not really sure what you're doing. It shortens the amount of time that they rattle on. It's brought attention to the fact that they have taken more time than they're entitled to.

—Kathleen Pence, Attorney

Reflective Journal

What did you discover about your habitual rate? How will deliberate or intentional use of rate variety affect your opening, closing, or questioning? What do you notice about rate variety in the speakers you hear? How do you as a listener or audience member react to speakers who use ample rate variety? How do you respond to a speaker who has a predictable rate, either too fast or too slow?

_____

_____

_____

_____

_____

Varying Volume

The women attorneys I admire most are real; they are very comfortable in their own skin. They have great eye contact, are confident and comfortable moving around the courtroom or presentation room. They have mastery of the facts and issues at play. They will raise or lower the voice to get jurors or others listening to focus on what they are saying.

—Laura Clark Fey, Attorney

Volume has to do with how loudly or how softly you speak. It relies on two factors in the body—breath support and space in the mouth. If you have been told you can't be heard, you need to increase breath support and open your mouth. Like pitch and rate, your volume needs to adjust and change through the course of your openings and closing in order to hold the attention of the jury.

Let's put volume on a continuum from one to ten, one being so soft, no sound at all, to ten, being so loud your listeners are covering their ears. Gauge appropriate volume level by what can easily be heard throughout the room, maybe a two or three; never go above eight and use that sparingly and deliberately. So the range of volume variety is between two and eight, using mostly four to seven.

It is helpful to enter the actual court space the night before or the morning of procedures to check the room for sound. Assess how low you can speak and still be heard; how loud can you speak before it becomes too loud? If you have a paralegal or co-counsel, try the room together. Speak at your two level. Can it be heard? Ask your colleague for feedback. Speak at your seven level and feel the amount of reverberation from the walls bouncing back to you. Revisit the Filling the Space exercise from Chapter 1 to remind yourself how to increase volume without shouting.

Once you have reconnected with deep central breathing, review the exercises for released jaw, tongue, lifting soft palate, and relaxing the lips. You will have more control of volume variety if the resonating spaces are relaxed and open.

Exercises: Volume Variety

Below is an excerpt from an opening in which we use the one to ten scale (one being the softest and ten the loudest). Possible volume levels are noted in the left margins. Read the sample out loud, varying the volume levels as indicated. It will feel forced, but you are practicing a skill that will settle down once your body learns how to shift volume levels.

5 When the floor gave way beneath him, Tony fell to the concrete 16 feet below.

3 Fortunately, Tony was only 19 years old and in very good shape, so he was able to land on his feet.

7 But he shattered his ankle.

6 Tony was rushed to the Emergency Room.
The doctors had to put a titanium plate in Tony's ankle to hold his foot together.

2 Unfortunately, postsurgery Tony's ankle got infected.

3 After several other procedures, a new surgeon was able to get the infection under control and the ankle healed.

5 Tony now has a limp.

4 He returned to work after all of those surgeries during which he was about six months off the job.

5 Tony's ankle will periodically swell and get stiff, but he deals with it.

Now speak the same sample shifting volume levels randomly.

Speak the sample above one last time, allowing the volume levels to settle in where they feel natural. Don't think about it too hard; just go. The other two attempts will shake loose your natural instincts for volume change.

Finally, pick up your opening/closing, choose either the numbering system or a simplified soft, medium, loud vocabulary, and explore volume variety with your own speech. Ultimately, you are creating an environment in your body and voice in which volume variety is possible.

As I reflect on the speakers I have directly encountered who catch the interest of their audience, both male and female, I first hear a warm vocal quality, a measured pace, variety of pitch, rate and volume, an ease of body, and a command of language carefully chosen to tell the narrative. I think of the actress Jane Alexander. As chairwoman of the National Endowment of the Arts from 1993 to 1997, she spoke with warmth, authentic power, and confidence as she advocated for federal funding for the arts. She was grounded, centered, and comfortable in her own skin. I remember feeling comforted by the sound of her voice, like we were in the most capable of hands. What effect would these vocal and physical traits have on a jury?

One of my dearest friends, Ruth Brelsford, an award-winning educator, has a voice and presence that takes over a room in the best sense of that image. She speaks with a deep sense of personal truth. She has a well-trained voice that is deep and resonant, possessing confidence born of years in the classroom, directing for the theatre, and political advocacy. When Ruth speaks, everyone listens. If she hadn't been an educator and activist, she could have been an incredible attorney.

Let's look at how the elements we have already discussed in this book apply directly to catching an audience's interest. A fantastic attorney is physically at ease and comfortable in her own skin. A body that is fraught with tension will never move with ease. Even if a speaker has physical issues that hamper ease of movement, she can maximize her range of movement by easy release exercises of stretching and shaking.

The expressive attorney has easy natural alignment—feet hip-width apart and weight evenly distributed, knees soft, long back of neck, shoulders relaxed and down. Her arms and hands rest easily at her side, until they are activated by a specific need to gesture.

And most importantly the expressive attorney's breath is deep and centered. From hours of intentional practice, her breath supports each word, each thought, each inspiration from her engaged mind and imagination. Imagine that you are this attorney. As you enter the space, you breathe slowly and deeply. As you prepare to speak, you breathe. You continue to breathe deliberately at each punctuation mark in your speech. Breath allows you to find a measured pace and gives you freedom to pause for dramatic effect. You will not feel the need to fill silences with umms, errs, or uhhs; your breath fills the pause, allowing you to consider what comes next. Your deep breaths allow the audience to relax and breathe with you.

You remember that the warm quality and compelling tone of an effective leader is created through resonance and enhanced vibrations, which come from space in the mouth. You remember to lengthen through the back of the neck, release the jaw and tongue, and lift the soft palate. The expressive attorney moves easily through her pitch range. In addition to natural inflection, you are aware that inflection communicates meaning. The organic and natural variety in rate of speech that you bring to openings, closings, and examinations are yours to use in the service of your intentions.

Hold these awarenesses and new skills in your voice and body as we move to higher-level skills discussed in Chapter 3.

Sidebar

I speak in a strong voice. I do not rush what I say. I had some great court reporters early in my career who trained me to have a good cadence that allows them to type what I am saying. I try to be as natural with a jury, courts and clients as I am when talking to friends and family.

—Beverly Atteberry, Attorney

Whiney voices don't work. And I can tend to have a whiney voice at times. Lower voices. . . . I think women have to work harder to have a steadier cadence in their voices. You don't want to sound emotional or excitable. It's important to be very zealous for your client, but calm and objective as well. I use lots of inflection in my voice—a lot of animation. You don't want to get that deadpan glaze from a jury when you have put them to sleep. It is important to make eye contact with them to see if you are, in fact, connecting. You have to work hard to keep that jury engaged and focused on your key points. You may want to move a little bit more. Your voice becomes more dynamic and varied to wake them out of that gaze and win their focus back to what you're saying.

—Valerie Evans, Attorney

Chapter 3
Capturing Their Hearts

Every jury is different and you have to keep them engaged.
You have to help them understand, through storytelling, through
your tone, your voice, and your body language that you are
honest, sincere and will tell them the truth. You can know your
case forward and backwards, but if you can't communicate in
a believable way, no matter how great the case, you will lose it.
—Esther Sanders, Attorney

Personal power . . . implies having an innate sense of yourself that
does not depend on what you think other people think, the ability
and confidence to find out or ask what you need to know to do your
job . . . the ability to listen to comments and criticism . . . to take
care of your own needs . . . to maintain your energy and sense of
self-worth.
—Meribeth Dayme[23]

LAURIE

Though this is generalization, I think about confidence in this way: "Men have all the confidence and not the skill to back it up, while women have all the skill and not the confidence that goes with it." I have seen this borne out many times over the years. When I was younger, male attorney colleagues, the same age as me, who say, "Oh, I can do this." I know they don't have a clue about what they are doing. In contrast I would say, "I haven't done that before, but I'm willing to try."

It took quite a while for me to feel confident and comfortable in the courtroom. But with experience, I began feeling, "Yes, I do know what I'm doing. I know that things are unpredictable, but I've handled unpredictable things before. So whatever happens, it'll be okay. Right?"

At the same time, it doesn't mean you have no anxiety or fear. Anybody who says they have no fear going into a trial is lying or doesn't care. At the point where you don't have any anxiety or concerns, it's time to go do something else. The confident lawyer walks in thinking, "Who knows. It's a crapshoot. Anything could happen. But I've got as much skill as anybody else. I can deal with what's coming my way."

I am aware of negative mental messages; it happens all the time. We give that voice so much power. "You're not as good as this other lawyer. You didn't spend enough time preparing." My counteraction is to meditate and to be in a place of calmness so I am not listening to that voice. You just get to the point where you can counter those thoughts with "That's not true. I'm not going to listen to you." Affirmations don't work for me. But being in a place where I'm calmer and more comfortable means that I'm not distracted by my own negative head trash talking.

Why is "capturing their hearts" important enough to deserve its own chapter? If you don't ultimately capture the hearts of the jury, they will not go into the deliberation room and take on the challenge of advocating for you and your client. Potential clients won't sign you to take on their case. Clients won't tell you the intimate details that could help you carry their case over the line. Most decisions are made from the heart and are often justified by facts but are made on a gut level first nonetheless.

In theatrical terms, the performer who captures the audience's heart is totally authentic. Her words are clear and deeply felt, and she speaks from the heart. The highly successful attorney does the same thing. It may seem like an ephemeral quality, a talent that you are either born with or not. I have worked with actors for decades, and I know that it can be taught. There are tangible skills, muscles at work in the body, thoughts in the brain, and ways of engaging the imagination that work together to impact the audience, jury, or potential client. The actor who transforms an audience is breathing deeply and is totally committed to each word she utters, each movement she makes contributing to her message. There is an ease with which she executes every moment; even when she is most fierce, she is connected to power in her center. In this chapter you will learn how to do the same.

Building Authentic Confidence

As we take up the topic of capturing their hearts, Laurie and I guide you through a series of exercises and discussions that will build on what you learned in Chapters 1 and 2. We start with authentic confidence because that is the foundation. Low self-esteem is a barrier, acting like a negative force field radiating out, keeping the jury, colleagues, and clients at a distance. Any lack of confidence manifests itself in the body as a form of "fight or flight," setting up conditions in the body and mind that block us from being completely present. When we are not completely present, the jury will not totally buy into us either intellectually or emotionally.

Fight or flight in this context can also be called performance anxiety or nerves, and it exists in all of us to a greater or lesser extent on a continuum of sorts, from no anxiety to total panic and dysfunction. But rest assured, the discomfort from stage fright and low confidence can be managed, even reversed.

My journey toward authentic confidence has been like a roller coaster ride—now I have it, now I don't. Sometimes it felt like a momentary loss; other times it was days, weeks, even months. When I made the move from teaching high school drama to higher education, I experienced a crisis of confidence. I truly felt I didn't belong there. "Who am I fooling, I am just a high school teacher, masquerading as a professor." I was apologetic and uncertain in all I said and did in my classes. Of course, the students picked up on this mindset and took me to task, pointing out missteps and misspeaks with glee. My end-of-term evaluations reflected their disapproval, one even saying, "She should go back to teaching high school." Ouch!

I remember fretting, stewing, crying, calling friends for moral support, and thinking I had taken on more than I was capable of. Over winter break, I did some serious soul searching. In the midst of this crisis of confidence, I was observing a fellow professor, Jack Wright, who was the epitome of the model college professor—beloved, talented, nurturing, but challenging; students scrambled to take his classes and audition for the shows he directed. While weeping and wailing, I started to ask, "What would happen if I acted as if I were Jack Wright?" Not pretend to walk and talk like him, but carry the ease and confidence that was always so much a part of him. In the spring term, I tried out my new resolve—to "act as if." And the students bought it! Almost immediately, their attitudes and behaviors toward me changed. I began to feel better, my confidence genuinely began to escalate, and I finished that semester with much stronger evaluations. I behaved in a confident manner and my emotions followed. My body led and belief followed.

I know I am not alone in this tale. Many of you have experienced times when your confidence failed you or you denied yourself an adventure, an opportunity, or a relationship because of lack of confidence. I am sure some of you make less money than you are worth because you lack the confidence to go after the raise or the promotion you deserve. The information and work that follow will take you through a process that develops both the mind and the body to build more authentic confidence.

What is confidence? What does it look like? Your list might look something like this:

Confidence has energy, joy, and focus.
Confidence shows no anxiety or fear.
Confidence lives in an open, relaxed body, where deep breath is flowing.
Confidence has a strong, clear voice without apparent effort.
Confidence is a synchronization of talent and skill.
Confidence takes risks, knowing that failure, though possible, does not kill.
Confidence is taking the jury on a journey from ignorance to knowledge, to feeling, to deep belief.

Reflective Journal

What is your definition of confidence? What would confidence look like in you? If you had all the confidence in the world and knew you could not fail, what would you do? What in your life drains you of confidence? What are your habitual negative mental messages that shut you down?

_____

_____

_____

_____

_____

_____

_____

As a gender, women are still experiencing a crisis of confidence. We only need to look at the ongoing pay disparity between men and women to see an example of this crisis. Yes, there is a real wage gap; but there is also a confidence gap. If a man and a woman are both looking at the same job description, a man will apply if he meets only 60 percent of the job's required skills, but a woman will not apply unless she has 100 percent of the skills. Women negotiate for a pay raise less often; and when they do, they expect less. In a room of mostly men, a woman will be reluctant to speak. A man in a room full of women will speak as much as he always does.[24] My dear friend and frequent co-presenter, Diana Morgan, gave one of our groups this advice:

> I think it's important to understand the dynamics of sexism and oppression so that we can better understand what we are up against and have compassion for ourselves. I don't think we are served, however, by focusing for very long on the injustices toward women. In fact, when I do so I become ill. I think the most powerful thing we can do is to use this information as a springboard into action, taking risks, speaking up, and growing our confidence. Women have come a very long way, and while there's still a long way to go, our fore-mothers and fore-sisters worked for the freedoms that we now enjoy. As a woman I feel a lot of freedom, and I am thankful for that. I intend to keep growing and risking, finding my voice and building my confidence.

To better understand confidence, we can look at the three components that together make up our confidence levels. Confidence is part biology. We come into this world with a predisposition toward or away from confident behaviors and feelings; it is in our DNA. There are three neurotransmitters that play a huge role in confidence: serotonin, oxytocin, and dopamine. Serotonin has the ability to inhibit anxiety. It helps us make calm, rational decisions because we feel less stress. Serotonin calms the amygdala, the fear center in our brain. Oxytocin, known as the cuddle hormone, generates warmth and positive attitudes. It creates the desire to hug, have sex, be generous with friends, share, and be faithful. It's heavily tied to optimism and paves the way for people to act and take risks. Because of our genes, some of us have more oxytocin than others. Dopamine, known as the adventure chemical, inspires doing and exploring, curiosity, and risk-taking. The absence of it creates passivity, boredom, and depression. Based on how our genes express themselves, some of us have more dopamine than others. When it comes to confidence, dopamine gets us moving; serotonin induces calm thoughts; and oxytocin generates warm and positive attitudes toward others.[25] So our biology can give us a kick start or a setback right out of the starting gate.

Confidence is also part nurture, which is how we were brought up. Did your parents foster or squelch confidence? Even if nature dealt you a weak confidence hand, nurture can shore you up. If your parents and teachers were dedicated to building your confidence by providing activities in which you could succeed, gave support and encouragement for you to take risks and helped you learn resilience when you fell short, you could thrive with a high degree of confidence intact. Our upbringing has a huge effect on our adult level of confidence.

Most important to understand for our work, confidence is also part choice. If both nature and nurture let you down, you will have some challenges in the confidence department. You can, however, overcome these challenges and build confidence. The brain is plastic; it is malleable and always changing. You can teach your brain to think different thoughts, to have different beliefs. New neurotransmitters in the brain can be formed through specific exercises and daily attention. You can practice to be confident, and if you do the exercises on a regular basis, your brain and your emotions will start to believe a new truth. You can override genetics and childhood environment. So life choices matter. Fairly simple brain training or methods of thinking can carve new pathways in our adult brains, pathways that encourage resilience and confident thinking and can become part of your hard wiring. Confidence is a choice we can all make!

You can make a choice right now to control negative mental messages that can drain your confidence. Write down your familiar negative messages. Then rewrite them as positive statements. For example: If you wrote down, "People will think I am stupid." Rewrite it, "People think I am smart and competent." Your subconscious will hear this and begin to believe it. New neuropathways will form and confidence will grow.

Reflective Journal

Write down the negative mental thoughts that drain your confidence.

_____

_____

_____

_____

(Continued)

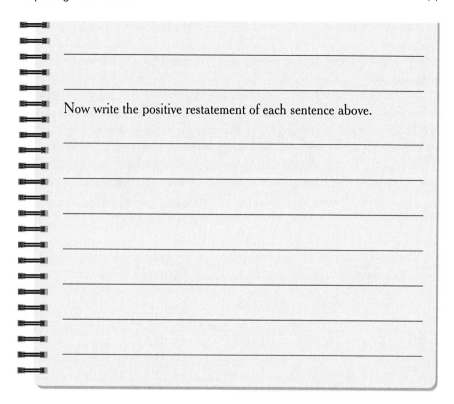

Now write the positive restatement of each sentence above.

Use these positive affirmations, out loud or silently, during your mediation time, when you are walking, jogging, or even brushing your teeth!

Taming Performance Anxiety

In Chapter 1 we learned the importance of breath for voice, but breath is also key to confidence building and taming performance anxiety. Performance anxiety is a fight or flight response to the pressure or stress we experience when speaking in situations that matter—in the courtroom, a deposition, delivery of bad news to a client, a media interview. Symptoms range from upset stomach to perspiration, dry mouth, shaky hands or trembling knees, shallow breath, tunnel vision, loss of vocal clarity or volume, and brain shutdown. These annoying and sometimes debilitating symptoms are caused by a chemical shift as the body prepares itself to flee or defend in the face of what it perceives as danger. When it is happening, we feel powerless to control it. We can, however, learn to manage performance anxiety so that it does not hinder our work.

The remedy lies in a little long-range preparation to help the body and mind deal with performance anxiety more efficiently and adoption of some simple pregame strategies to gain control of the symptoms.

When I have a major speech or seminar, I start preparing the night before by having a light healthy meal, not too much wine, a little yoga, and a good night's sleep. The morning of my event, I do a workout or at minimum a physical warm-up that involves stretching, shaking, and deep breathing. At points throughout the day, I try to stay connected to deep central breathing. Shallow, rapid breathing can signal the onset of, or actually cause, fight or flight. Control your breathing and you control the chemical shift. Below are two breathing exercises that calm, quiet, and focus the mind and body.

Exercises: Taming Performance Anxiety

Slower, Deeper, Quieter, Calmer

Sit comfortably in a chair with both feet flat on the floor and your eyes closed. Begin to focus on the breath by thinking "slower, deeper, quieter, calmer." Feel your breath slow down, on both the inhale and the exhale. Feel your belly moving in and out easily with the breath. Each in-breath goes deeper into the torso. You should hear no noise as you inhale or exhale. Feel, and with each breath, you get calmer and more confident. Your shoulders relax, your jaw releases. Repeat for ten breaths.

Four, Seven, Eight Breath[26]

Sitting comfortably with eyes closed as you did before, inhale for four counts, gently hold the breath for seven counts, and breathe out for eight counts. Repeat at least five times.

These two exercises will help to ground and center your breath, your emotions, and your body energy—the foundations of authentic confidence.

Exercise: Visualizing Success

Have your opening/closing ready to use at the end of this exercise.

- Still sitting comfortably, with your eyes closed, breathing slowly and deeply, tune into the sounds around you. What do you hear close to you? Imagine there is a circle of sound near you. What do you hear all around you in that circle? Extend your ear a little farther and imagine that the circle is larger, farther away from you. What else can you hear in this outer circle?

- Tune in again to your breath, in several slower, deeper, quieter, calmer cycles. Now imagine yourself in the upcoming professional situation, trial, negotiation, deposition, judge's chambers—whatever might cause you anxiety or a loss of confidence. See yourself shining with success. You are telling your client's story with clarity and expressivity. Visualize in detail what that looks like—standing strong and firm, confidently using your voice, asking clearly for what you want. Imagine everyone listening to you attentively. See what are you wearing, what are the surroundings, who else is present, and hear the words you are saying. Feel power and ease deep in your center; breathe for several moments until it feels familiar.
- Continue to breathe slowly and deeply. As you bring the visualization to a close, open your eyes, stand, ground yourself, and speak. Feel the ease, confidence, and energy in your center. Be aware of any shift in how you sound. This ease can be yours, each time you need it, by going back to this visualization exercise. You can do it the morning of an event, or a few minutes before, as you warm up your body and voice in preparation to bring your best self fully to the task at hand.

Reflective Journal

Nothing builds confidence better than action. Make a list of actions, both large and small, you can do, which perhaps you have not had the confidence to do before. Maybe it is picking up the phone to make that call, volunteering for more responsibility, or talking to a colleague about a challenging issue. Push yourself out of your comfort zone. Choose one a week to tackle, and then mark it off your list. If you are feeling brave, choose one a day! Celebrate the doing regardless of the outcome. Small successes work together to build confidence. Big victories are made from the accumulation of small ones.

_____

_____

_____

_____

(Continued)

_____

_____

_____

Celebrating your strengths: Create a list of the positive
traits you possess. Celebrate your strengths as part of your daily
meditation.

_____

_____

_____

Write out the accomplishments you are proud of. Read
them out loud or use them in meditation.

_____

_____

_____

Meditating Daily

Meditation does work! It alters the chemical makeup of your system,
producing calm and reducing fear in the brain and consequently
throughout the body.

Laurie and I collaborate with Lexlee Overton, founder of Mind Over
Law, who is a trial lawyer, mindset expert, and Energy Master. After years

as a successful trial lawyer, she suffered from professional overwhelm and burnout and decided to explore ways to be a better lawyer without sacrificing her mental and physical well-being. She traveled the world studying how the mind works and learning mindfulness and energy mastery techniques. Drawing from the fields of psychology, neuroscience, and energy medicine, she has created empowering practices that help lawyers be the best versions of themselves, by teaching them how to defeat their fears, trust their intuition, decrease stress, and remain calm and bold in their presence both in and out of the courtroom. Of the stress of the law, Lexlee says:

> The practice of law is unlike any other profession. We argue and fight for a living. Each and every day, we are immersed into conflict and competition. We work long hours, live under constant demand to be on top, and our clients depend on us to be top notch. There is no room for mistakes and the pressure of practice comes at a high price physically, mentally and emotionally. In our field, stress and anxiety are considered a given. Burnout? Just part of the job. But what if that weren't really the case?
>
> Breath focus commands awareness in the moment. Long, slow, deep breaths have a dual purpose of connecting the mind and body along with detriggering the central nervous system stress response. When we are locked into our fight or flight response, we often breathe at a chest or thoracic level, which contributes to many physical problems like rapid heartbeats and low blood oxygen levels. The 7 Breath is a powerful stabilizing and releasing practice. This tool has many benefits, including:
>
> - Detoxifying the body by releasing carbon dioxide and other toxins
> - Correcting the anxiety, panic, and hyperventilation of shallow breathing
> - Triggering the body's relaxation response by stimulating the parasympathetic nervous system, creating a calming effect
> - Increasing energy levels by increased oxygenation boosting metabolism[27]

Exercise: Seven Breath

Stand or sit comfortably, eyes open or closed, breathing in and out through the nostrils.

- Begin breathing in on a slow count one to seven.
- At the top of the inhale, take a brief pause for another count of seven.
- Begin slowly exhaling while counting from one to seven

- At the bottom of the exhale, hold the breath out for a count of seven.
- Continue the full inhale and exhale pattern for at least three minutes.

If you are not in the habit of meditating, it may feel awkward at first. But a few minutes every day will make a lasting change in your authentic confidence and general anxiety level, helping you find your inner powerful woman while feeling more peaceful and grounded.

A young woman was in a seminar audience as I shared the voice and confidence work outlined in this chapter. Several days after a two-hour presentation, she emailed me this success story: "My lungs were filled with gratitude as I gradually released the love during a brief appearance for a news feature. Because of what I learned at your presentation, I humbly welcomed the opportunity to speak in front of a camera. I practiced as much as I could remember from your session for the brief televised interview. I remembered to align my body, keeping my chin parallel to the floor, mindfully grounding my feet, and did many rounds of the 4–7–8 breathing exercise to relieve my nerves!" She attached the news clip, and she was just lovely.

As I stated earlier, confidence is built through taking small risks and succeeding. The young woman in the story above took a risk. With some new knowledge and a technique, she prepared, took a small risk, and succeeded. Look for small challenges in your professional realm, lay the groundwork for success through preparation, and raise your hand. Then celebrate your success. Don't let your habitual negative mental messages tell you, "It was just a fluke." Counter that with, "I was successful because I am good. I prepared and I succeeded. I can do it again."

To this point we have been focusing on our inner world, thoughts, and emotions that underpin confidence. Let's switch gears now and look at the physical elements that we can easily control. In acting training, we teach that emotion comes from action. When we put our body in confident postures, a confident feeling follows. What does confidence look like on the body? Grounding and centering are components of both confidence and taming performance anxiety. Grounding starts with feet in solid connection with the floor—feet hip-width apart, weight evenly distributed. A person who is not grounded and centered will never be perceived as having confidence. Natural alignment is also a component of confidence. From the feet, natural alignment moves up to a long back of neck, soft front of neck, shoulders relaxed and down. Deep central breath is a component of confidence. All these systems intertwine and synchronize to make you the best version of you and firmly secure your authentic confidence without the discomfort of performance anxiety.

Owning the Room and Presence

Presence as a personality trait is a term that floats around in professional circles. We know it is a marketable trait, a great quality to have; but the definition of presence feels illusive, vague, almost undefinable. If we don't have it, an even bigger mystery is how to get it. Presence is part of confidence, yes, and just like confidence, it can be developed.

I can recognize presence in others. Like confidence, natural alignment, grounding and centering, and deep breathing are part of the story but by no means the entire story. What if a person is physically limited in some way—does that mean she cannot be present? Clearly, that is not true. Even if illness or accident impairs alignment, there are many examples of present, even charismatic, spirits that are housed in compromised physical frames.

Eye contact is part of presence. A present person makes a connection with eyes that really see. Yet as I say this, I think of Olympic weightlifter, author, and motivational speaker Jim Stoval, who is also blind. I don't ever recall feeling more seen and understood than I did in the presence of this generous and accomplished man. He made a connection even though his physical eyes could not take me in. He was hearing me, sensing me, and seeing me. His mental focus was on me, not on himself. Even though I had requested the meeting to interview him about his professional speaking career, he was curious about me, asking me question after question before I could even open my notes. As I left his office, I recognized that I had received a gift, not only of his time and information, but of his presence as well.

Presence then, at its core, is an outward focus. Energy flows from self to others. Others' needs are more important than our own inner chatter which competes for our attention. It takes daily commitment to listen and observe. An actor's trick I learned in drama school is that when your internal monologue is deafening, you need to observe something specific about the other person. See the person as if for the first time, as if you must memorize every feature of that person. The more you focus outward, the less you will focus on yourself.

Owning the room is taking confidence and presence another step and opening it into the space to include all who are in it. To own a room, you "first must read it. Sensing the mood, absorbing the cultural cues, and adjusting your language content and presentation style accordingly are vital."[28] When you are able to own the room, you no longer focus on yourself; you focus on the needs of others.

I have recently added the word "sparkle" to my definition of owning the room. It is in the eyes that says, "Ready, excited, let's go!" It is a glow of energy that flows out of the individual and embraces the entire room.

Exercises: Presence, Owning the Room, and Radiating 360 Degrees

Highly successful attorneys have something extra, something that is often called **charisma**. They seem to radiate warmth, confidence and energy. You, too, can learn to radiate warmth, confidence, and energy—in all directions!

Start with grounded and centered alignment. Feel your feet firmly connected to the floor and your knees soft. To be centered, feel that your energy source is located in the area of your navel. Breathe deeply and centrally. Your shoulders, neck, and head are released. You are making easy eye contact with the space around you, taking in your surroundings and really seeing them. Your level of performance anxiety is low and your level of joy is high.

- Stretch your rib cage, patting your ribs to encourage deep release.
- Find your feet, soften your knees, and feel the long back of your neck, the soft front of your neck.
- Connect to a deep central breath by finding abdominal release.
- Release your jaw and keep your lips gently closed.
- Feel energy and focus coming out through your eyes, as if your eyes have laser beams. Don't squint or try too hard to manifest this feeling. Just feel that your eyes illuminate whatever you are looking at.
- Shift the focus of your attention to your center, and imagine that energy is flowing from your center. You have a superpower that is housed in your center. With each breath it gets stronger. Your eyes and your center radiate warmth and confidence.
- Now send your focus to your back. Imagine that you can breathe in and out through your back. Then picture a group of supporters who stand behind you, giving you strength. You don't need to turn your head to see them; you sense they are there—your breath and your radiating energy can touch them.
- Speak a few sentences of your opening/closing and imagine your voice easily flowing out your back to the supporters who stand behind you.
- Bring awareness to your rib cage. Feel each inhale expand the ribs. Bring awareness of space into the rib cage. Imagine that your rib cage is

aglow with energy. Your superpowers are not just in your center and your back, but also in your ribs.

- Speak again and feel your ribs radiate with sound energy.
- Imagine a glow of light all around your body—a thermographic image. As you breathe, feel your image becoming stronger and clearer. Be sure you have not picked up tension in your knees, shoulders, upper chest, or jaw.
- Say your speech again, imagine that your whole body is an amplifier; sound comes out all around you, managed from your center. Don't let tension creep into your knees, shoulders, neck, and jaw. Continue to breathe deeply and make space in your mouth.

Carrying Confidence and Presence into Your Words

As you practice your opening out loud, your confidence will grow. At each practice session, be sure that you remember to:

- Ground the feet, soften the knees, lengthen the back of the neck, and find the moment when the inhale becomes the exhale.
- Speak your opening out loud and breathe at each punctuation.
- As you speak it again, image that you have been granted extra confidence from an unseen power. Feel that power low in your center.
- Speak it as if your life or your client's life depended on it. As you dial up energy in your center, keep your upper chest and shoulders relaxed and down.
- Speak it to an imaginary audience—the jury—and trust that they are going to believe in every word you say.
- Then just say it. Don't think too hard about doing it right—just release it!

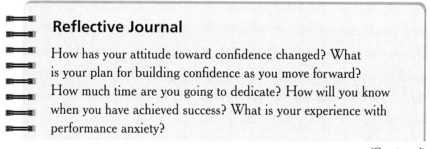

Reflective Journal

How has your attitude toward confidence changed? What is your plan for building confidence as you move forward? How much time are you going to dedicate? How will you know when you have achieved success? What is your experience with performance anxiety?

(Continued)

How are you going to manage performance anxiety as you move forward from this moment?

_____

_____

_____

_____

_____

_____

Sidebar

I have a great team, and one of the things I love about being a business owner is that it gives me the chance to create an environment that reflects my authentic self and my authentic values. I am making the space for other women employees to be that as well. I think we have the unique ability as a team to make our clients feel comfortable, loved, and appreciated. We are leaning into that, embracing that as a strength, and it has been deeply gratifying. It was literally at the ten-year mark in my career before I felt I knew what I was doing and quit questioning my own abilities. I now feel more empowered to take bigger risks and be more proactive. My focus is on serving my clients in the best way possible.

—Brittany Littleton, Attorney

I advise young women to challenge themselves. Try different things as often as possible and learn from those experiences. You must take risks and break out of your comfort zone to grow confidence professionally and personally.

—Cheena Pazzo

I was 40 when I was "yanked up" the corporate ladder. Within just three years of leaving Norman, Oklahoma, I was on a company jet three days a week. I never got on the jet that I didn't think, "They are going to figure out who I am and send me home." Every day I was on the edge of my comfort zone. It was scary on a regular basis. We must have resilience and tenacity. We have to challenge the status quo and assumptions. It may seem insurmountable, but, in reality, we can do this, one board room at a time, one relationship at a time. We have to be prepared to keep up.

—Teri Aulph

Making Words Matter

An actor captures the heart of the audience with words. Words are not accidental. They are chosen with care to elicit just the right response. Just as a playwright tries on many words before deciding on one, so lawyers structure words with similar care. We must learn to deliver them with the same care and precision with which we chose them. I have found that attorneys, in a desire to stick to the facts, often leave their hearts at home. If we want to capture the hearts of the jury, we have to bring our own heart into the courtroom. This does not mean being emotional or losing emotional control. It means connecting on a deeper level with what you see and feel so that your listeners see and feel as well.

Let's start with key words—nouns and verbs. They need to carry more weight, time, and attention than adjectives, adverbs, articles, or pronouns. Crucial to drawing and holding the jury's attention is the attorney's ability to communicate how she feels about the key words and what she imagines when she says it. Take the word "mother," for example. If you have a special relationship with your mother, if you loved her very much and have wonderful memories, when you say the word "mother" it carries with it all the weight of your feelings for her. If your relationship was troubled, fraught with tension and conflict, and left you feeling disappointed and unloved, when you say "mother," it will have a whole different feeling and tone.

So when you speak a noun like "ghetto," you see the image of what you mean in your mind's eye. What specific ghetto do you want the jury to visualize? If you see it, they will see it as well. The weight and importance you gave that word will stimulate their emotional memory.

Verbs carry action, so you need to give the verbs action. I don't mean this literally. But if you say, "He panicked," make panic sound like what it means, what it feels like. In a phrase like "Buried the body," make buried sound like what it means—deep in the earth with sweat and extreme effort.

Exercise: Key Words

Try these sample sentences:

1. John <u>adored</u> his wife Betty, and he was <u>devoted</u> to their children.
   a. Read the above sentence once without interpretation; just read the words.
   b. What does the word "adore" mean to you? Who do you adore or who adores you? Say the word "adore" with one of those images in your mind. It is a feeling verb and you want the jury to feel that too. You have to feel it, not punch it, but genuinely feel it.
   c. What does the word "devoted" mean to you? Who are you devoted to? Where in your body do you feel the emotion of "devoted?" Now say the word.
   d. Say the whole sentence making "adored" and "devoted" sound like what they mean. Again, don't punch it up unnaturally. I am just asking you to feel what that word means to you as you say it.
2. They built their dream <u>home</u> on the top of the <u>hill</u> with a full <u>panorama</u> of the green <u>countryside.</u>
   a. Read the sentence once without interpretation. Just say the words.
   b. Focus on the word "home." Say the word as if you were standing in the middle of your dream home. What does it look like? See it. How do you feel? Say the word again. By envisioning a specific home and allowing yourself to have an emotional response to it, you will endow it with power to make the jury envision theirs as well.
   c. Say the word "hill." What is the most beautiful hill you have seen? Imagine it in detail as you say "hill."
   d. Do the same with "panorama." Let the word itself carry the weight of the panorama that you envision. If you make the word matter more, it is a little longer in length and may be elevated slightly in pitch. Don't *make* it do any of those things. Simply see the image and have a response to it as you say it.
   e. Finally, explore the noun "countryside." How do you feel when you are in the country? In your mind's eye, create the lushest countryside you can—maybe with wildflowers and velvety grass, or a forest's green canopy. Now say "countryside" as you see your vision.
   f. Put the whole sentence back together with your deeper understanding of what the nouns mean and how they look to you.

   Go back now to your opening or closing.

1. Underline the action verbs.
   a. Take the time to explore each one, out loud. Ask yourself the simple questions I posed in the above exercise. What does it mean, really? What action is being evoked? Say the word like you mean it.

    b. You chose just that word and no other word. What do you want the jury to feel? Say it again so they can feel it too.

    c. Read the entire speech with a new understanding and sense of the weight and importance of the action verbs.

2. Circle all the nouns; the words that identify objects, places, people, animals (that which can be seen, pointed to or made plural). Take each noun one at a time. Picture the thing. Is it beautiful, wondrous? Say it as such. Is it disgusting, horrible, destroyed, or gone? Say the word; make it sound like what it means and what you want the jury to feel in response. This is not to make you overly dramatic or inauthentic. It is to help you be truly authentic with a real experience of the words you use.

3. Go back to the top and say the whole speech. Don't punch the key words; let them be what they want to be as a result of the exercise. Notice if the key words have more specificity now, more power and detail.

Inspiring Imagination with Action Verbs

Using action verbs is a well-trusted acting technique that keeps an actor grounded in authentic objectives, goals, or motivations. It also helps to inspire vocal and physical variety in an authentic way. Action verbs help you clarify your objective. An objective is defined as what you want to do to or get from the person(s) you are talking to. For every moment you speak, whether to the jury, the judge, a witness, your client, or colleague, you want to achieve a goal; you have an objective. The more specific is your goal, the more detailed and expressive is your voice.

We do this in life. Every moment of our interactions is guided, even driven, by what we want to achieve, our objective for that conversation. When speaking to your children, your objective might be to comfort them or to punish them. How you speak and relate to them is dependent on your objective. When you are interacting with your partner or spouse, your objective could be to support and to lift up or to deflate him or her. The movement of your body will vary depending on that objective. Your voice will also respond differently in rhythm, rate, volume, inflection, and tone quality, depending on your desired result.

Although we do this unconsciously in life, we can consciously apply objectives as we speak in legal situations. Notice that all the above examples carry implied action. To discover what your objective is at any given moment, ask yourself, "What do I want to do to, or get from the jury, right now?" Then jot it down in the margin of your speech. These action verbs become your interpretative roadmap through an opening or closing.

Below is a list of objectives, stated as action verbs, which an attorney might find useful.

to scare	to flatter
to accuse	to shame
to warn	to calm
to comfort	to mollify
to empower	to cheerlead
to coax	to punish
to inspire	to placate
to torment	to defend
to save	to dissolve
to lure	to convince
to educate	to shock

Having a clear objective or intention in mind will help you authentically intensify the emotional effect that your words will have on the audience.

Exercise: Using Objectives and Action Verbs

Look again at your opening/closing. Read the first paragraph out loud. What effect do you want this information to have on the jury? What do you want to do to or get from them? What is your objective? Look at the list above and choose one. Connect with deep central breathing and place that objective in your center—this is what you want to do to the jury; believe it in your core. Then speak the paragraph. Get your eyes off the page as much as possible. Imagine the jurors' eyes locked on yours.

Notice what you felt, what you sounded like. Was there a difference in rate, volume, or tone quality?

Look at the list again and find another verb that stimulates your imagination. Connect with your deep central breathing and place that objective in your center; this is what you want to do to the jury. You can even say to yourself or out loud, "I want to inflict shame" or "I want to warn." Believe it to your core. Then speak the paragraph. What do you notice about how you feel? How is it different from the previous verb image? What happens to your voice? Do you feel your body adjusting in any way?

If your speech is four to five minutes long or longer, you will want to assign an action verb to each section, paragraph, or topic. The first section could be to scare, the second section to warn, and the final section to empower. Write your action verbs in the margins. Actors call this "scoring the scene." These images will inspire you to find different tones, rates, volume levels, and emotions that will lend variety and interest to your speech.

Objectives and action verb imagery not only help with authentic variety but also force focus away from yourself and onto the jury. To be truly authentic, your focus must be out of yourself and onto others. It is about them, not about you. The minute your focus comes back to you, self-consciousness rears its ugly head and you cease to be effective, sponta-neous, and natural. You become instantly less compelling in the eyes of the jury. The magic happens when your attention is placed outward watching others, not inward watching self.

Using Eye Contact

There is nothing more attractive than a person with shining,
sparkling, fully present eyes. . . . Eyes with a light in them show
life, energy, awareness, and a reflection of a physically, mentally
and spiritually healthy person.

—Meribeth Dayme[29]

When we are capturing hearts, eye contact is a crucial weapon in our arsenal. The moment of eye contact, really seeing and being seen, can be powerful and transformative. It is a crucial part of being fully present and building true rapport. The jury needs to feel that you see them, as does a client or a colleague. Eye contact communicates, "I am here. We are in this together. I see you," which at base is what all of us need in any meaningful relationship. It makes people feel valued and important. It also conveys confidence and competence.

Eye contact can also be tricky, and for some, it is quite difficult. There are no hard and fast rules that say "eye contact now, eye contact not." But, I am going to share with you what I have learned from my own experience, what is generally thought to be true by the "experts" and some recommendations from practicing attorneys on the subject.

When presenting to a group, pick one person to look at for the length of a sentence, and then pick out another face to speak to for the length of the next sentence. Some speakers use the 180-degree eye-sweep, which takes into account the full view of the room through your peripheral vision. This is a good way to establish the comfortable limits of your eye contact range. The danger here is that it can give uncon-scious permission for your eyes to sweep from one side to the other without ever really seeing any one person.

In one-on-one conversations, eye contact moves naturally to the other person and then away. I try to make eye contact when the other person is talking. When I am talking, part of the time I make eye contact and part of the time I gaze away momentarily to find a new thought.

Observe the use of eye contact in the conversations around you to see how natural eye contact works. We can get hints about how to use our own bodies by observing how others use theirs and seeing what is effective and what is distracting. Excellent speakers and presenters are dedicated observers of life around them, always watching for how people use their bodies, their gestures, and their eye contact when they are not self-conscious.

Some speakers have a habit of looking at the floor to get their next idea. Know that anytime the audience loses your eyes, they lose connection. When you are gathering your thoughts or thinking about what's next, use a sightline slightly above the heads of the audience to refresh your next thought.

Yes, there can be too much eye contact. If you stare constantly at one person, it can be creepy. Mostly I find, however, the need is for more and better eye contact. Although I am pretty good generally with eye contact—it is easy for me, I love people—I do practice it intentionally when I am working up a speech.

When I coach clients, I will ask them to look at me, use me as a real audience member. "Tell that to me." Or I stick "post it" notes at three or four spots on the wall and ask the client to speak to the spot as if they were faces in the audience. I coach "one pair of eyes, one sentence." I finish the thought before moving on to next set of eyes. I place objects or chairs in the room to represent members of an audience.

It is a default habit to randomly gaze over the heads of the audience and hope they feel they have made contact with you. Your eyes must meet their eyes. If you are uncomfortable or, because of habit, just not good at it, you can solicit friends or colleagues to help you. Ask them to sit and be your audience. Give them permission to tell you how well you established real eye contact with them. If you really struggle, you can extend your hand to a member of your practice group. Hold her hand as you make eye contact and only let go when you have finished the thought. Move on to another person in the group and extend your hand to them. As you make eye contact speak to the end of the thought. Encourage them to let you know if you made solid contact with them or not.

When practicing a speech, if I allow my eyes to glaze over, the same thing will happen when I am in front of an audience. Performance is the result of remembered rehearsals, so practice as you want to perform. And that includes eye contact.

Reflective Journal

When you tried "making words matter," what did you notice about your voice and emotional connection to the words you use? Which of the action verbs drew out variety in voice, body, and inflection? What are you aware of in terms of eye contact? What have you observed in your use of eye contact? What will you add to your personal process to better connect with your audience?

_____

_____

_____

_____

_____

_____

Sidebar

Eye contact is imperative. But you have to use it purposefully. I tell my students, in voir dire and in opening, that they have to make visual contact with each and every juror. If they don't, they've insulted that jury. The fact is that jurors, even if they're uncomfortable with eye contact or they're introverts, want to feel important. So you have to make connection with them. If you have to pause and wait for that person to look at you, you pause and look at that juror. During questioning, the only time I really look at a jury, although I'm always watching them, is when a point is made. I will physically look at the jury as if to say, "Did you hear that? Did you see that?" It is a form of an exclamation point. I always make sure to use strong eye contact when I'm arguing to a judge. I'm not looking at my notes. I'm not fiddling. I want to be sure the judge knows if I'm saying something, by God, it's important.

—Shena Burgess, Attorney

I use eye contact pretty deliberately much of the time. If my opposing counsel's rattling on, I will either stare at the judge or at the attorney and wait for them to finish. I avoid eye contact with the opposing party because I'm not allowed to talk to them, so I act like they're not there. I don't want to be construed to have somehow engaged with them. In a deposition, you also have to be aware of eye contact. Sometimes your witnesses will look at you when they get a question, like they want a prompt. I typically sit right next to them. I can see them look at me, but I won't look at them at all. I don't want to spark a response like, "Let the record reflect counsel smiled at their. . . ." So I don't look at them at all until there's a break in questioning. I've had clients, or parties, throw their hands up and look at me as if to say, "What do you want me to say?" No response. I literally just sit there and stare at them. Stare at them or look at the other attorney. I can't show a response.

—Kathleen Pence, Attorney

It is crucial to connect with the jury—to be someone jurors can relate to and trust. I have found it to be effective to vary the volume of my voice. I have observed that thoughtful pauses and silence can be very effective in the courtroom. Eye contact is also critical, as is natural movement through the courtroom.

—Laura Clark Fey, Attorney

Eye contact can be more communicative than words. If a witness is being difficult, steady and firm eye contact can make them shift their position.

—Rebecca Newman, Attorney

Building Suspense

Suspense is defined as "a condition of mental uncertainty or excitement, as in awaiting a decision or outcome, usually accompanied by a degree of apprehension." In theatrical terms, it is "anticipation of the outcome of the plot or of the solution to an uncertainty, particularly as it affects a character for whom one has sympathy."[30] We enjoy suspense, particularly if the uncertain outcome is not about us. For a jury to want to go the distance with us, we have to build suspense. Some people believe the circumstances of the story provide the suspense. But it is actually in the storytelling where the audience is drawn forward to the edge of their seats, waiting for the resolution. There are certain delivery techniques that can help the lawyer build suspense in the jury.

The truly effective attorney uses rate and pitch variety, as well as a well-placed pause, to build suspense. For example, you are about to deliver a primary point which you want to imprint in the minds of the jurors. You can build up rate, getting faster as if headed to a cliff. Then take a pause that feels like a suspension, followed by a drop in pitch as you slow down the rate to deliver the coup de grace. This can maximize the dramatic effect of that detail, making it more likely the jury will retain the information.

A silence or pause can be very effective either before or after key information. Look at this sample sentence:

> When the floor gave way beneath him, Tony fell to the concrete 16 feet below. Fortunately, Tony was only 19 years old and in very good shape, so he was able to land on his feet. But . . . he shattered his ankle. He was taken to the emergency room.

Try the pause after the word "but," making the audience wait for what is to come. Then slow way down for the rest of the phrase, "he shattered his ankle." Go back to a moderate pace for the last sentence.

Try the same sentence again, this time, taking the pause after "ankle." Let that information hang in the air for a two count, then deliver the rest of the information.

> When the floor gave way beneath him, Tony fell to the concrete 16 feet below. Fortunately, Tony was only 19 years old and in very good shape, so he was able to land on his feet. But he shattered his ankle. . . . He was taken to the emergency room.

Judge for yourself which feels more effective. Write in where you deem the pauses should go. Be careful that you don't pepper your speech with pauses. Save them for the truly big moments.

You can score an opening or closing by circling those moments that you want to heighten and clarify. Read them out loud. Try various ways to handle them. You can go from slow to fast, loud to soft. You can explore where the pause might work best. It is only through exploring and practicing out loud that you find the most effective way to build the suspense.

As we discussed earlier, making the words sound like what they mean is another way to build suspense. If, for example, the sentence is "The defendant then stabbed my client." You did not say "nudged," or "nicked"; you chose that word to have impact, so allow it to do so. You can ask yourself a series of simple questions as you practice making words sound like what they mean. Say the word again in answer to each question. For example: "How would it feel if you were stabbed by a random passerby?" Your answer is "stabbed," as it grows out of your emotional response to the question. Another question: "How does it feel to imagine a blind child and her service dog?" Does it perhaps "stab" at your heart? Say the word again with that image. Another question: "How would you feel about 'stabbing' a point a during a cross-examination?" Say the word again, with stabbing a point in mind. Now say "stabbed" in the context of the original sentence: "The defendant <u>stabbed</u> my client."

To simplify these questions, still using the sentence above and the word "stabbed":

- Ask yourself, what is your worst experience of the word? Visualize the answer but say only the word "stabbed."
- What is your best experience of the word? Visualize again and answer with the word "stabbed."
- Finally, give the word as a gift. Say the word again as you present it as a gift: "stabbed."
- Read the entire sentence, "The defendant stabbed my client."

The word will be enriched and colored by the impact of each question. You don't need to push or try too hard, the explorations you did will serve you in an authentic way.

None of these suspense-building techniques should take you into "melodrama land." Even though I encourage you to go all out in the exploration phase, ham it up a bit; ultimately, you just have to say it like a real person. It will carry an authentic ring with just the right amount of expressivity. Make a video recording of yourself and watch objectively for building suspense in a natural way.

Sidebar
Juries want it to be interesting, as interesting as it is on TV. So I try to create theatrical storytelling, not huge drama theatrics, where it is appropriate. It holds their attention. I start with my outline; then I fill it in. I try to tell it from beginning to end in a format that people can follow. Ideally, I'd spend more time videoing it, practicing it over and over, to discover what notes to play. It's not just about the words. It's about how you're saying it, and making sure that you're bringing that drama in at the right moment, heightening the clarity of the points you want them to remember.

Eye contact is important, and you must connect by looking at them. Everybody wants to feel important. However, jurors don't want you staring at them for too long, so don't overdo it.

You have to find the right distance between that witness and the jurors. If you want them to focus on the witness, you stand closer to the witness. If you don't want them to focus on the witness, you step away from the witness.

—Esther Sanders, Attorney

Acknowledging Characters in Your Story

One of the things that a good attorney does is to humanize her client. We want to evoke understanding and compassion for the key people in the story. What are some ways to accomplish this? We have already explored the importance of key words—nouns and verbs. We know how to make words sound like what they mean. We have learned that rate, pitch, and volume variety help us to tell a story in a way that will draw in a jury.

I'd like to add one more strategy to our toolbox—characterizing. In acting, an actor transforms herself into other characters. The actor's body, voice, and imagination become those of another person. In the legal setting, the flexible attorney may give a "nod" to characterization by using a subtle change in voice and body language to give the flavor of the character discussed or described—not by becoming someone else but by sparking the imagination of the jury. When used in conjunction with these other techniques, the jury is more likely to sympathize with you and your client.

For example, read the following paragraph out loud:

> Ben was 12 years old when he was crippled. Without any warning sign, he did not have the experience to know the small black wire was dangerous, so he is not contributorily negligent for doing what all young boys do—playing in a field near his home.

Read the sentence out loud again, from Ben's point of view, but not by becoming the 12-year-old Ben. Just try softening your voice or raising your pitch slightly, giving a nod to his childlikeness. You are simply evoking the innocence of the child, and the jury will do the rest of the work.

No matter who the character is, your voice and body language can give a gentle nudge to the jury as to how they should feel about the person being described or discussed. Here is another example. If you are talking about a "bad guy" named Robert Smith and you have a whole paragraph about his "badness," you are likely to harden your voice and maybe lower your pitch.

Read the following paragraph out loud as strictly neutral facts.

> And how did the ungrateful Smith thank May? At the end of twenty years, he claimed a right to use May's stairwells forever. And he claimed the right to May's water, forever. When May said that wasn't ideal, he sued May. Proving no good deed goes unpunished. But there is more. Smith wants the right to use the exits and the water in the garage without paying for it. And he wants to do this forever. He wants something for nothing.

Read the paragraph again, making Smith a total villain, overact, have fun. This man is a scoundrel.

Read it one last time, with just a nod or a slight indication to Smith as a bad dude. On a scale of one to ten, a ranking of ten means you are "chewing up the scenery" with Smith's badness. A ranking of one means he is a total saint. A ranking of five means Smith is neither bad nor good. Read the paragraph at six or seven, leaning into his badness, giving a nod toward the negative. It is very subtle but effective.

Memorizing the Story in Pictures

I coached an attorney who had an extremely complex story to share in her opening. She was practicing her presentation with a focus group and got lost several times, unable to remember what came next. In the theatre we call this problem "going up on your lines." She lost her place because she had tried to memorize word for word and there were just too many words. She looked at me panic-stricken. I dismissed the focus group and took her to her office.

I asked her to read the first paragraph out loud. I asked, "What is the picture you want the jury to see in their mind's eye from the information in this paragraph?" She described it. Then I asked her to draw that picture. After some resistance ("I can't draw") she made a rough sketch of the details she wanted the jury to understand and see. I held the drawing up in front of her and said, "Describe this picture." She did with ease and clarity, omitting no important detail. I taped the drawing to the wall.

Then we went on to each paragraph or section and drew the pictures. We taped them in succession around the office. Next I asked her to tell me the opening by describing each picture she had drawn. She was able to remember the whole story by describing the pictures in an authentic, spontaneous, and compelling way. The mind can remember a series of pictures easier than it can a very long series of words. In addition, the act of drawing more deeply embeds the information in your brain.

Sidebar
The women attorneys I admire and respect most have a quiet confidence, not overplaying any aspect. Women have to be very careful about that. I think men get away with raising their voices and being more dramatic than women can. There are a lot of labels that get thrown at women if you don't have certain boundaries with your voice, your presentation—steady, calm but confident, respectful and firm.

In dealing with a jury, the most important thing I have learned is that you had better be honest. Do not stretch anything. Do not ignore anything. Do not sidestep anything. If there is a problem with your position, your case, or your client, meet it honestly head-on. I represent plaintiffs who obviously have had some sort of misfortune, and we wouldn't be there if we didn't think somebody should be held accountable for that. Most jurors think they would have made a better choice and would have done something differently that would have prevented the misfortune. You have to meet those head-on and try to give them an explanation of that and why this happened; they did their best and nobody else could have done much better. That's crucial in getting a jury to sit in your client's seat.

A jury must trust you and think you're being honest with them; you must be sincerely yourself. And to do that, you have to stay within who you are. You can't be someone else.

Even if you see someone who you think is very effective, if it is not your nature to speak that way, or to project that way, or move around the courtroom, or stand still, whatever they're doing, even if it's somebody you admire greatly, if you are not comfortable, the jury will know it.

So as you move forward in your career, number one is to be comfortable in your own skin. Part of what helps me is being ultra-prepared. If you're fully prepared, you are more confident and calmer. You're always going to get curveballs; but if you are prepared, you can react calmly to them.

—Lisa Riggs, Attorney

Preparing and Practicing

There are as many ways to prepare as there are attorneys preparing, but there is uniform agreement that prepare you must. This includes openings, closing, voir dire questions, deposition questions, direct and cross examinations, and presentations. Some women report that they write it out word for word and then distill it to outline form or bullet points.

Some use notes in presentations, some don't. Many rehearse in front of focus groups, some in their office, some in the car, some as they walk or hike. But you must practice out loud. David Ball and Joshua Karton in their book, *Theatre for Trial*,[31] advise practicing in the actual courtroom or conference room the night before, if possible. Hearing the words in the space will increase your comfort level and help you know how to gauge the room for projection and clarity. Your practice run-throughs will always feel a little self-conscious and not quite as natural as you do when the adrenaline and focus of the actual event kicks in, but trust that your body and brain are learning and synapses are forming. As awkward as your practice runs feel, they are making your presentation better.

A Rehearsal Process

From years of coaching actors to, in the last four years, working with attorneys, I have found that simply saying it over and over, without a focus for each run-through, can reinforce ineffective delivery habits. What follows is a process for giving each practice-run specific intention. If you follow the sequence below, the final result will be compelling, authentic, and polished, including all the aspects that we so carefully practiced in Chapters 1 and 2.

- Read through the entire speech just to say all the words. You will notice sentences that are awkward or too long. Rewrite as necessary.
- Read for breath. Check into the rhythm of your natural deep central breathing, feeling the "moment of readiness." Read the speech and breathe at each punctuation. Remember that you shouldn't say more than seven to nine words on one breath. This is for your audience's benefit—they can only take in seven to nine words at a time before they need you to take a breath. If your sentence does not have enough punctuation, find places for them or mark breaths at phrase or thought changes. Your body needs to memorize where the breath happens just as it memorizes the words.
- Now that you know where all the breaths go, read it again, connecting breath to thoughts. Think about what you are saying as you breathe at punctuation.
- Yawn, massage the jaw, release the back of the tongue, lift the soft palate. Read the speech again, making a large, easy space for vowels. Enjoy the vowels. Vowels carry emotion. Give them space and time.
- If tongue-speak is effective for you, read one sentence or paragraph in tongue-speak and then say the same sentence or paragraph with your tongue back in your mouth. Go through the entire speech in this manner.
- Then just say the speech and be aware of added ease and clarity.
- At a two volume level, not a whisper, just low volume, speak your speech again, stressing every consonant, every final t or d, as well as beginning and middle consonants. Feel and enjoy the consonant energy.
- Now say it again. You should notice greater ease and clarity.

- Circle the nouns. Read the speech and physicalize the nouns. That can be a gesture or a large abstract movement. Don't think about it or plan what you are going to do; just do it. The more full-bodied you make this gesture, the better.
- Read it again and see if the nouns take on more importance and specificity.
- Circle the action verbs. Read the speech and physicalize the verbs to give them life and physical commitment.
- Say the speech again, and be aware that key words, nouns and verbs, are more alive. You shouldn't have to punch them or manufacture their importance. They should just feel natural as they take their place of easy importance.
- To make sure you are not dropping off at the ends of sentences, as you speak the speech, point your figure on the last word of each sentence.
- Score the speech with an action verb for each major section: to warn, to scare, to inspire, etc. (Refer to the action verb list presented earlier in this chapter.)
- To get the whole body engaged, try an imaginative run-through. You can do Master Thespian, Pitch Absurd, sing it, or dance it. The point is to vocalize and physicalize with abandon.
- Finally, ground and center, connect with your breath, and speak your speech. Let it happen naturally. Believe in it, believe in your goal of bringing the audience with you. It should feel and sound like you—an improved, clearer, more expressive version of you.

In this chapter, we have covered a wide range of topics in order to capture their hearts. Think of each exercise and each topic as spokes of a wheel, all attaching at the center, which is your goal of emotionally connecting with jury or client. There are a lot of spokes going to that center. You will find the ones that resonate with you, that feel comfortable and move the work forward. Take on those that do and set aside those that don't.

Ultimately, these are all practice techniques. When you actually speak in front of a jury, you want to release all the work and focus on what you are saying, trusting that all the work you have done in practice will sustain you. Techniques are useful only if they help free you to be your best authentic self. Remember to breathe as you wait, breathe as you listen, breathe as you rise; find your feet, soften your knees, feel the long back of your neck, breathe into your center, and speak from your heart!

After the trial, deposition, or presentation, celebrate what you did well, and acknowledge what still needs work. Let yourself off the perfection hook. Your public presentation persona is always a work in progress.

Sidebar

In preparation, I start with a very detailed, typed-out presentation that includes literally all the words I want to say. I practice it out loud over and over, standing and moving around. I time myself to see how long it is. Do I need to cut it? I try very hard to pace myself and breathe; I don't want to go too fast. Just to remind myself, I write in my outline, "Take a breath, pause." If I have demonstrative exhibits, I put them up. I'll get in a conference room so that I can move to them and point out what I want. Once I get comfortable with the full script, then I pare it down to a short outline with a few highlighted words that I keep with me as a security blanket so I don't get nervous or lost. I hardly ever have to use it, but having it there allows me to communicate directly with the jury.

—Lisa Riggs, Attorney

I practice openings and closings in my head and out loud, in the shower, before I go to bed, while driving. Your opening is the first time you lay out your narrative, your theory, who your client is, and what you want them to talk about. If you don't lay it out there, 80 percent of the jury has already made their decision. I think about tone of voice. Do I need to speak faster? Slower? Am I going to be aggressive with this witness? I think about every single aspect. You have to plan it out for each witness, opening, closing, everything. I plan out my wardrobe for the entire trial. For voir dire, I'm going to be in a neutral, light brown or a light gray because I want to be approachable. When cross-examining a major witness, by God, I'm wearing the red suit. I plan it down to the color scheme. I don't wear pants in jury trial. I may have an older male or female juror, who doesn't think that women should be wearing pants. Am I going to offend them by my clothing and jeopardize my client over something that little? Most of my trials have been murder trials. I have someone's life in my hands.

—Shena Burgess, Attorney

Chapter 4

Amplifying Story with Body Language and Gestures

Body Language used in concert with your well-crafted message and voice is a powerful persuasion tool. Nonverbal communication includes your stance or seated posture, poise, eye contact, overall energy, gestures, and facial animation. Body language nonverbally communicates feeling and meaning.

—Rebecca Diaz-Bonilla[32]

The body is always communicating, whether we are conscious of it or not. Often the message our body sends is not the one that we intend. Sometimes our bodies send messages that obscure what we are saying. How you walk, how you stand, where you carry your weight, how you sit, where you focus your eyes, how you use your hands, and the tilt or lift of your head all communicate something about you. Even the smallest details of physicality tell viewers volumes about each of us, leading them to form opinions, both positive and negative. The body speaks its own story, apart from our words. Although specific studies differ on the actual statistics, it is safe to say that well over half of what an audience knows and understands about us is derived from our body language. It is ironic that many speakers spend hours writing and practicing a speech and then just hope the body will come along for the ride. Esteemed leadership coach Kristi Hedges says that "your actions underline or undermine your presence."[33]

In order to ensure that our bodies work *with* us rather than *against* us as we speak, this chapter explores unique ways of understanding how the body works. We will look at large and profound truths about how the body is organized to create meaningful communication; we will also discuss how to manage and use the body to tell compelling and convincing stories. We want our bodies' stories to become just as deliberate and conscious as the stories we tell in words.

Michelle Obama is a superb example of an authentic, skilled speaker who uses her voice and her body to make a connection with her audiences, both large and small. When she walks on the stage, there is no doubt that she owns it: she is at home, easy, relaxed, and fully present. Notice her natural alignment, her confident stride, her grounded and centered stance. Before she even opens her mouth, we know from her body language that we are in capable hands. She moves with ease; her authentic gestures support her message. David Oats, president of Stalwart Communications, observed, "While Mrs. Obama used prepared remarks, she presented them with genuine sincerity and emotion. She believed in what she was saying and the audience got that. She was confident, not cocky . . . she had her eyes on people, not prompters. . . . Instead of focusing on the screens, Mrs. Obama made sure she engaged the people in the hall at a personal level."[34]

LAURIE

The magic of the movement and gesture work that Rena teaches was brought home to me as I was working on an opening in a complicated product liability case involving fireworks. The key evidence was the audio from a video recording, and it would require the jury to listen hard to hear the distinct pattern of the normal sound of a firework being lit and engaging and the slightly different sound of the firework we alleged was defective being lit and engaging. The evidence was there, in the sound, but trying to educate the jury as to these minute differences was going to be a challenge. After struggling with it myself and with other lawyers (who were the first ones who caught the different sound), I brought a rough draft opening to Rena. I had tried to vocalize the different sounds and educate the jury early as to what to listen for. But it still wasn't coming across all that well.

In Rena's studio, we worked on adding movement to the delivery of this description. Suddenly, the opening became much more powerful and engaging. When gestures are clear and specific, story is amplified.

To get your body ready for easy, confident movement and gestures, you need to warm it up by loosening and releasing habitual tension, as described in Chapter 1. Attend to each body part, starting with head and neck and then moving through the entire body, stretching and breathing. Yoga is a great warm-up. If you enjoy dancing, turn on your favorite music and rock out, releasing tension and raising your energy level. Our bodies love to move; the more we move them freely, the more likely they will be there to organically support our story.

Opening and Closing: An Exercise for the Body

Bodies that are open and released give the impression of being present and accessible; bodies that are closed off because of habitual tension look awkward and inaccessible. If shoulders are high, you look stressed and anxious. If shoulders are forward, you look tentative and lacking in confidence. If shoulders are back and held, you project harshness, inflexibility, and aggression. Shoulders that are relaxed and down communicate a sense of being grounded, present, and confident. An open body radiates energy outward; a closed body is constricted and armored, stifling energy.

The following exercise will help you feel the difference between an open body and a closed body. Think of "open" and "closed" on a continuum—moving from the most open to the most closed. In this exercise, we will move back and forth slowly from open to closed, allowing you to experience sensations in the body and at various points on the continuum. As you move through this exercise take care of your body—moving as fully as your body allows.

Exercise: Opening and Closing

- Start in natural alignment. Be aware of the breath in your center.
- Widen your stance to shoulder width and extend your arms above your head so that you are standing in a giant X. Extend your arms and feel the energy coming from the floor up your body and out your hands, breathing deeply into your center as you do this. Be aware of how this feels throughout the body.
- Now round over, curling yourself into a small ball, holding your muscles tight, closing yourself. How does this feel?
- Then extend into your giant X again, feeling power and openness, and breathe deep into your center.
- Curl into a ball, closing yourself again.
- Go back and forth between open and closed, at your own pace, eight more times.
- Return to natural alignment: feet hip-width apart, knees soft, pelvis balanced, spine easily lengthening, head floating on top of the neck, chin

parallel to the floor, shoulders relaxed and down, and breath dropping into your center. Hopefully, you feel easy strength, a tingling of energy in the body, and ready confidence. This probably feels similar to the grounding and centering exercise or increased internal awareness from Chapter 1. This physical state should become your baseline, your default. Whenever you speak, whether in court, depositions, or consultations, this is where your body starts—open, spacious, and free.

Moving the Right Amount

I am often asked "How much should I move?" "Do I move too much?" "Is it boring just to stand there?" No matter what you do physically, stay grounded, centered, and open. If you feel compelled to move or gesture, make sure it reinforces what you are saying. A listener will always follow gestures over the spoken word, so random movement quickly becomes distracting. When it comes to gestures, less is usually more.

Vanessa Van Edwards, lead researcher at Science of People and author of *Human Lie Detection and Body Language 101,* says that audiences see hands first. We might say we notice the eyes or smiles; but, no, it is really the hands. This is a primitive instinctual response to register the presence of danger. "Does this person have a weapon that could kill me?" This places extra burdens on our gestures. What are our hands doing that add to or diminish our message?[35]

It is my hope that after doing the exercises outlined in this chapter you will start to feel more comfortable using gestures. When I am coaching speakers who truly don't know what to do with their hands, I will choreograph a few telling gestures and encourage practice until they feel natural. You can also keep your hands relaxed at your sides. I tend to keep my hands up, at about waist level as though my elbows are resting on the bottom of my rib cage. You can also gently rest them on a podium, not leaning or gripping. You can easily hold your notes in one hand, keeping the other hand ready to gesture if need be. If your hands tend to fidget, hold a pen if that will ground you. Resist the temptation to click or tap. The pen can become part of a gesture or a pointer.

LAURIE

I don't know about this one, Rena. All the lawyers I've seen do this are distracting. They can't resist playing with it. Very annoying.

Point taken. As a theatre director, I have often given an actor a single prop, like a pen, to distract from a greater problem of nervous hands, or worse, dead hands. But you have seen way more trials than I have. It may well be a crutch that our women can learn to live without.

If you use your hands a lot, make a video of yourself and watch the playback. If you are moving your hands all the time, simplify! Pick the gestures that communicate something specific and stick with those. Ask a friend to watch your presentation and give you feedback about gestures. Encourage your friend to be honest and specific.

At your best, you should not be consciously aware of your hands. If you are prepared, if you stay on breath, if you are focused on connecting and clearly telling your story, your hands will do what they need to do. They will reveal your inner emotional world. If emotions are open, hands will be open; if emotions are closed, hands will be closed. If you release habitual tension and do some opening and closing, you will start to feel more confident and comfortable, and your hands will begin to look more comfortable as well. Think of your body movement and gestures as extensions of your thoughts, there to support and clarify your message. Voice, body, movement, and gesture are all part of your storytelling instrument.

Pacing

Some speakers are always on the move. If that is you—stop! It is more important to remain grounded and centered than to constantly move. If you are in front of a medium-to-large group, you may want to think of your movement pattern in terms of a triangle. Center front is the starting point. If you have a major transition in the subject matter, you can take several steps to the right or left and find a new person to talk to. Then stay put for several sentences. On another transition or subject change, you can look to the other side of the room and take a few steps in that direction. Then stay put until the next transition, which takes you back to center. You have made a movement triangle. In a five-minute speech, one pass of your triangle, or three movements, is all that is necessary. Major movement comes at thought shifts only, transitions, or subject changes. Gestures are used to reinforce a point, to illustrate, or to enhance energy—never just because you don't know what else to do.

As I suggested earlier, a video recording of your practice or presentation can be a great learning tool. You will notice which habits or mannerisms are effective and which are distracting. Recently, I watched the recording of one of my presentations, and I noticed how many times

I readjusted my scarf—I no longer wear scarves when I speak. I also became aware that I habitually tuck my hair behind my ears—I now spray my hair back so I won't be tempted to play with it.

LAURIE

For me it is dangling earrings. I have stopped wearing them when I speak. If they distract me, I am sure they distract the jury.

Your goal is to be the best you can be, learn from your mistakes, and make changes. Don't punish yourself or dwell on your mistakes; just notice, practice, and grow.

Reflective Journal

Once you have that recording, look at your body language. Observe your gestures. How often do you gesture? Are you grounded? Do you sway, or shift weight frequently? Do your gestures enhance your message? Do you look comfortable? Do you seem confident? How is your alignment?

_____

_____

_____

_____

_____

_____

_____

Video #8: Gesture Circles, Gesture Shapes
(Access the video at www.myvocalauthority.com/hervoiceinlaw.
Enter the access code: HerVoiceinLaw1212.)

Using Gestures

Gesture Circles

Movement Specialist and dear friend, Matthew Ellis, shared a movement paradigm with me that has proven invaluable as I begin to talk body language to clients who have not done much physical work. He talks about the body in terms of circles and shapes. Circles are regions of the body from which movement originates—there are three of them. The first circle is our lower abdomen, where survival instincts reside, where sexual energy is centered, where need for food and shelter take root. The second circle includes the stomach, heart, and lungs where tenderness, love, vulnerability, hurt, and loneliness are housed. Finally, the third circle includes the throat, mouth, brain, and eyes where our intellect, words, and sense of humor are focused. All authentic movement or gestures come from the body, from an impulse or a need that originates in the body, and specifically from one of these three areas, energy centers, or circles.

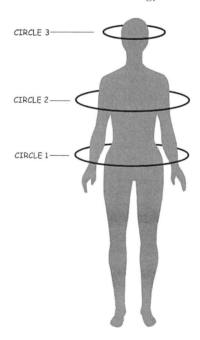

Three Gesture Circles

In Circle 1, if I am talking about base instincts, survival, deep fear, or a violent act, my center of energy will be lower in the body, and a gesture will also remain low at my waist and closer into the body.

Gesture from Circle 1

In Circle 2, if I am speaking of love, disappointment, or compassion, my heart center is activated and my gestures will be at chest height.

Gesture from Circle 2

In Circle 3, if I am speaking of something I know in my mind to be true, or I want to appeal to the listener's intellect, my gestures are going to be higher in the body. The hands are closer to the head, mouth, or throat.

Gesture from Circle 3

Exercise: Exploring Gesture Circles

• Create a set of three gestures that feel comfortable for each circle. Link them to a sentence or phrase.
  Examples:

  "She did as you would do, she fought to protect her child." Circle 1
  "Your heart must break when you hear these details." Circle 2
  "Please think before you decide." Circle 3

Create phrases that you might actually use in a speech or use one of your existing openings or closings. Then explore a gesture that goes with the phrase. Practice speaking and gesturing at the same time. If you discover one you believe might work for you, even if at first it does not feel natural, repeat it over and over until it does. Record yourself; you can tell if a gesture looks natural and adds to your message.

Gesture Shapes

Gestures also have shape in space: triangle, square, and circle. A triangular gesture shoots out from the center like an arrow and is pointing out, attacking, accusing or directing attention toward. "He did it."

"She sits there before you." "It started with her." "That woman right there." Practice a triangular gesture, pointing to an imaginary witness as you say each line. Make the gesture with confidence and clarity; feel energy extending out of your index finger.

Triangle-Shaped gesture

In the square gesture, hands are parallel and palms face each other. The square is immovable. "This is the situation." "Let me explain it this way." "For our purposes today." A square gesture can be close in or farther out; high near Circle 2 or lower from Circle 1. Practice each sample sentence above and try a square gesture with each. Repeat enough times until it feels easy and authentic.

Square-Shaped Gesture

For a circular-shaped gesture, the hands move in a circle. It could mean taking and giving back. "Here is for you, here is for me." "All of us are in this together." "This is true both before and after." Try a circular gesture with each of these sample sentences. Try different ways to realize the circle. Find the variations that work for you.

Circular-Shaped Gesture

Exercise: Exploring Gesture Shapes

- Practice a triangular gesture for the following phrases:
  "I would not be here today if not for her."
  "You, my friend, are wrong."
- Practice a square gesture for the following phrases:
  "All of the evidence leads to this conclusion."
  "What I offer here will save you time and money."
- Practice a circular gesture for the following phrases:
  "This is a mutually beneficial agreement."
  "This process is on-going."
  "This should startle all of us."

Exercise: Putting Circles and Shapes Together

Go back to the video you made earlier as you examined your movement patterns. Watch it again, observing how you use gestures in light of this new information on circles and shapes. Choose a gesture you observed yourself doing in the video. Is there room to clarify and sharpen, making the body circle clear and more dynamic? Can you make the gesture shape more distinct? Practice the gesture as you say the sentence. Repeat several times.

Go back again to your video. Focus on gesture shapes. If you point for any reason, are you pointing with clarity and conviction? Is there an opportunity for a square gesture? Pick a sentence and try a square gesture. A circular gesture is probably the most challenging. Look for language that reinforces consequences—"as a result," "in order to," "if you do that, this will happen," or the circular nature of a relationship—"first you, then we" or "this builds on that." That kind of language cries for a circular gesture. If you identify words that are similar to these examples, try a circular gesture.

Think back to when you learned to ride a bicycle or first took up golf or tried to perfect your tennis serve. The first ten attempts were probably pretty rough. You may have felt awkward and uncoordinated. But if you persisted, your parent let go of the back of the bike and you pedaled forward, or your club made solid contact with the ball, or you hit the serve gracefully over the net! As adults mastering body language, we may want to give up the first time a movement feels awkward. With practice though, these movement concepts can be mastered and the physical map of your presentations can be award-winning.

Reflective Journal

What do you notice in terms of your movement? When do you look relaxed? Is there a point when you look uncomfortable? Which gestures support and reinforce what you are saying? Are there any that are distracting? Can you eliminate the ones that don't add to or support what you are saying? In light of the information regarding gesture circles and gesture shapes, what do you see in your own gestures? Are you using the three gesture circles? Do they match up with your choice of language? Which gesture shapes do you use most frequently? Are there opportunities to employ other gesture shapes?

_____

_____

_____

_____

Sitting

We have spent a lot of time discussing movement and gesture, but you probably sit more than you stand. Sitting is an insidious energy sucker. How you sit can focus your energy and attention and send it out to the room; or it can dissipate your energy, making you look and sound weak or disinterested.

Let's look at some messages you may be sending by the way you sit in a chair. Conference rooms often have swivel chairs that are such fun and soothing. Don't swivel back and forth randomly; it diminishes your strength and gravitas and is distracting from your message. Only swivel to get better eye contact with someone at the other end of the table. If it is too great a temptation, lock it off.

If you cross your arms over your chest, you close yourself off from the others. If you lean back, you look disengaged. If you lean forward and make eye contact, you look engaged. Sitting forward in the chair slightly can convey interest. It is also easier to access deep central breathing which keeps the brain in gear. Sitting too far forward can communicate that you are ready to attack or take over. Resting your head in your hands can convey boredom. A pen poised to take notes says, "What you are saying is important." Tapping or clicking a pen says you are jittery, bored, or distracted.

Try sitting comfortably in natural alignment, long back of neck, soft front of neck, shoulders relaxed and down, breathing deeply, one or both hands resting easily on the table. This conveys confidence and presence and will help you to feel that way too.

Walking with Confidence

How do you walk into a room? Do you convey confidence? The work we did with natural alignment is directly applicable to our discussion of how you walk. Let's take a moment to contrast your familiar walk with your natural or confident walk. Take note of how you walk to your office from your parking spot. How wide are your strides? How do your feet come in contact with the ground? Where are your neck and head in relation to your shoulders? Where are your arms? How much or how little do they move at your side? If you carry a backpack or a large purse or briefcase, how does that affect your alignment?

A great actor exercise is to observe how others walk and try to put their walk in your body. Malls are great places to people-watch. Staying at a discreet distance, follow someone and then see if you can move as he or she does. Trying on other people's walks makes you more aware of your own. It also teaches you how flexible we truly are. Make it part of your practice to observe other people. Ask yourself questions. Do they project confidence, bluff, or denial (to use terms from Chapter 1)? Are they healthy, happy, sad, or lonely? All this you can learn from watching someone pass by you.

When you enter the courtroom, a deposition, a meeting, or a presentation, how do you carry yourself? Is your stride balanced? Not too wide, not too narrow? Do your feet land easily, moving heel to toe? Are your shoulders relaxed and down? Do your arms swing easily at your side? Is your neck long with chin parallel to the floor? Is your jaw relaxed? Are your eyes switched on and alert? Are you breathing deeply and centrally? This is your confident walk. Practice as you walk through the mall, as you walk from your car, or as you walk down the hall. This is just natural alignment in motion.

Clothing as Body Language

What you wear is part of body language as well. There is, of course, no pat answer for this one. Professionally appropriate clothing varies by region and by individual style. It is a balance of what feels authentic to you, how you want to present yourself to the world, and what your clientele will not find distracting. If an adornment is offensive to a potential client or members of the jury, are you willing to risk alienating them for the sake of personal expression? The women attorneys I interviewed vary widely in their thoughts on this issue. Several report that they wear suits with skirts, and some only wear pants suits. One said red power jackets for sure, and a few said black, navy, or gray. One mentioned that well-kempt and flattering hair styles and make-up are a priority. Most agreed that avoiding the provocative or sexualized look of too low or too short is a good rule of thumb. When you are younger and making your mark, erring on the more conservative side is recommended so that you draw attention to your skill and knowledge rather than your looks. As your reputation develops and your skills sharpen, you can afford to be more yourself, if you are inclined to more flamboyance. Keep jewelry choices simple and tasteful. I love multiple bracelets, but they clink together when I gesture, so I forgo them when I make presentations.

We have covered a wide array of topics in this chapter. Everything you do communicates something, so body language must be deliberate. The bottom line is awareness, observation, and practice. Simply knowing that sitting, standing, walking, and gesturing are part of your storytelling arsenal is step number one. Observing deeply how others move and gesture widens your own options for movement. And finally, the more you practice, both specifically and generally, the more adept you will become at using your physical presence to amplify storytelling. If you practice any sport, body work, or physical movement, continue. If you don't, make it a part of your life. It doesn't have to be intense and exhausting; it can be yoga, dancing, walking, or bicycling. Use your body in an intentional way and it will support you as you move through all professional situations.

I physically run through my trial before I try it. I think about every single aspect. You have to plan it out for each witness, opening, closing, every-thing. I think about positioning, where I am in the courtroom, what I'm doing during jury instructions. Am I going to be by my client? How many times do I interact with my client? Do I put my hand on my client's shoul-der? Especially if it's a client the jury may think is scary, if I put a hand on a client and the jury sees it, they're going to think, "Oh, she's not scared of him." If I want the jury to look at my client, I go stand by my client and make sure the jury's focus is on me and the client. Or I ask the client to stand. You know they're going to look at him then.

—Shena Burgess, Attorney

My body language is not soft enough according to a lot of people. I started in the legal profession in the early 1990s. I was told by male and female attorneys that I needed to wear lower heels, wear more masculine suits, and have shorter hair. I ignored them. I have always preferred dresses and high heels. I have long hair. I keep my clothes and hair neat and well kept. I purchase professional clothing that I know I will be able to wear for twenty years. Our society has become so relaxed that some of my younger colleagues do not know how to dress for a professional career. It does not mean expensive or boring; it does mean that they should not get mistaken for their clients in a courtroom. It does mean that they are not in clubbing clothes or looking like they just got back from the lake. The successful col-leagues I most admire use their bodies naturally and are true to their own personalities. They do not apologize for who they are or what they fight for.

—Beverly Atteberry, Attorney

Chapter 5

Applying Voice to Everyday Situations

It was through my collaboration with Laurie that I began to see all the various legal situations and scenarios where the voice and body work can be subtly integrated to achieve enhanced performance and better outcomes. I am often asked the question, "How do I apply this work to my professional life?" In this chapter, Laurie and I address this issue, sharing practical tips and strategies for applying these new skills in your professional life.

LAURIE

Concern about the voice is not limited to litigation—pretrial interactions, transactional situations, all have unique communication demands. As a civil lawyer, whether you are on the plaintiff's or defendant's side, we typically have structured events—mediation or arbitration or a settlement conference—all of which use some kind of intermediary, so generally we don't have the opportunity to speak to the other side. We are speaking to the intermediary and hoping that they will carry the message we want to the other side. So it is an exercise in persuading somebody who is supposedly neutral.

In other contexts, if you do criminal work, the defense lawyer is negotiating directly with the district attorney or whoever is making decisions on that side of it. The two of them are negotiating directly. They don't have the intermediary. Sometimes in civil work, you can pick up the phone and speak directly with attorneys or insurance adjustors. Much of it is one-on-one communication. In all of these situations, it is crucial to remain grounded. I find that part of the job stressful;

probably because you don't have much control. I don't know what is going to come at me or what will be offered.

Actually listening and hearing what is behind what they are saying are also most important. You are on high alert during that time. If you are ever going to have a "gotcha" moment, it is in this context. "Wow, I didn't see that coming." That makes it stressful. When you are triggered into fight or flight, it can make the voice go strident, you lose the ability to be spontaneous and flexible. The less experience you have, the more likely you are to have that reaction. Plus, in a lot of those situations, you are doing it in front of your client. So now you have an audience. I am stressed, inside I am freaking out, and the person I am working for is sitting right here, perhaps losing trust in me. So if you are practiced at controlling voice and body and using them as a tool, as opposed to an obstacle, you have a better chance of a positive outcome.

Non-trial Work

Most attorneys spend much of their time in non-trial pursuits. As a matter of fact, even trial cases rarely see a courtroom. Many women are finding that being in business for themselves, either as solo practitioners or in smaller boutique law firms, is preferable to big law. This usually means that you have to secure clients.

LAURIE

Looking at the bigger picture, potential clients fall into two broad categories and require two different approaches. Plaintiffs' attorneys deal with injury or tragedy. Typically then, these potential clients are in states of heightened emotional vulnerability and must be handled with empathy and care. Outside of litigation, you may be soliciting in the area of probates and trust, again handling people's emotions and expectations. You will be talking to people about things they don't want to think about, and yet you must convince them that they need your service. Family law, of course, is always heavily charged with emotions. In these situations, you need to lead with empathy, trust, rapport, and authenticity.

In my practice, in the initial consultation, I hear their stories—something horrible has happened, and this may be the first time they have told anyone on the outside. They really want and need to be heard. It is more about being present for them and listening than about what I can do for them. At the same time, there is this counterbalance. You get a percentage of people who, given the opportunity to let go, will go on and on. They could talk about their situation the whole day, but I don't have that kind of time. So how do you give them the space to say what they need to say without letting it consume all your time? How do you show empathy so that they feel they have been heard? By the end of that meeting, I want that person to feel I "get" them. If I have to cut them off, I will say, "I need to focus on certain facts that help me figure out if I can help you." If they are going off on a tangent that doesn't help me make that decision, I need to rein them in. It is a delicate combination of being empathetic and assertive.

There is a second broad category of analytical, fact-based, less emotionally charged situations in which potential clients are seeking a different kind of support from their attorney. These potential clients—often a corporate client or an insurance company—want to get the best deal possible; emotional vulnerability is not an issue. You may be dealing with the general counsel or the in-house attorney who needs facts and process points, and want to know how you can solve their problems.

In an analytical meeting, typically, empathy is not an issue, at least not an obvious one. Early in my career, I was working at a defense firm, and we were trying to get the public-school insurance carrier as a client. Usually in that scenario, the task of getting new clients falls to the partners and not the young lawyers. But none of the partners had been educated in the public schools; they had all gone to private schools. They needed someone who had gone through the public-school system, so it fell to me. It was an obvious attempt to communicate, "We are like you." In that analytical meeting, they are looking for someone who understands their business. The clients you are seeking have experience in hiring employees or personnel, and they bring that experience into hiring a lawyer. They think they know, but often they don't. So you have to gently but clearly guide them into understanding why they need you and how you can help solve their problems.

Insurance companies, on the other hand, typically have tons of experience hiring lawyers. So their approach and needs are different. They frequently think that they know more about the litigation and legal system than the professionals they are hiring. This, of course, can rub the professional the wrong way, which can produce a delicate dynamic. You can get into a real battle of wills in that situation. If you want their business, you have to honor their ego needs and still be true to what you offer and how you work.

Selling Your Services

Laurie has outlined for us the two broad categories of potential clients and has suggested the types of language, treatment, and information they need to make the decision regarding whether or not to hire you. I know that many attorneys don't view themselves as salespeople, and selling services feels tacky to them. It is a fact of life, however; we must get clients.

I was an educator all my adult life. Until I started my consultancy four years ago, I had no idea how to frame a conversation or guide an outcome to signing clients. I do enjoy networking, which is just meeting people; I do that well. I have attended a lot of networking meetings and have had lots of coffee "to get to know you better." The whole procedure was also fun, but I wasn't signing any clients.

I then started attending a weekly sales training session taught by Robert Johnson of Bold Networking.[36] His "non-salesy" sales techniques suit my personality and feel authentic and flexible. These techniques have changed the way I approach selling my services. With Robert's permission, I now share them with my clients. Below is a brief outline, an oversimplification really, of how you might approach a meeting with a potential client. The points I am sharing are the ones that seem appropriate to selling legal services.

Let's start with the first meeting, the process whereby we determine if this will be a match—if they want me and if I can indeed help them.

- **Arrive grounded**, centered, and warmed up, whether you go to them or they come to you. Prepare to bring your best self to the meeting. Review the release of physical tension warm-up in Chapter 1. Make sure you are breathing deeply and centrally. Potential clients will respond to you if you are relaxed and comfortable in your own skin.

- **Establishing trust and rapport:** People like and trust other people who are like them. The technique of mirror matching can be very effective—giving back what people are sending out. If their energy is high, you can notch up your energy level; if their energy is low, modulate yours down a point or two. If they are casual, you can relax into casual; if they are professional and more formal, pay attention to your level of formality as well. How fast are they talking? How much are they gesturing? What is their body language doing? How are they sitting? It is not being inauthentic to mirror what they do; it is attending to where they are and meeting them there. Successful individuals are aware of, and flexible about, the energy, voice, and body language of the people with whom they are interacting.

- **Agree on a mutual agenda:** Clarify the parameters of the meeting to honor their time and expectations. "I want to respect your time. I have set aside an hour for this meeting. Is that still good for you?" "I know we discussed this on the phone, but can we review what your goals are for this meeting today?"

- **Use disarming honesty:** "I am not sure I can help you, but let's have a conversation and figure it out together?" Give them permission to say no; it takes the pressure off. People don't want to be sold, even if they have come to buy. Try some version of, "At the end of our conversation, it is okay to say no; it won't hurt my feelings."
- **Do your discovery:** Ask questions before you give your resume. "Tell me about your company (organization, yourself)." "Why are you here today?, "Why did you call me?" "What are your goals for litigation?" "What would be a good outcome for you?" "Tell me about that." "Uhuhh." "Go on." Draw out their real issues, needs, and pain points. Often, what people lead with is not the root issue. The more information you gather, the better able you will know if you can help them.
- **Paraphrase what you hear them say:** "Let me see if I understand . . ." Reflect the needs and emotions you've been told: "I can feel how hurt you are (or angry, or devastated). Who wouldn't be? I would be too." "You're needing to . . ." "You're concerned about . . ." It not only reassures them that you "get them," but also lets you know if you are indeed understanding.
- **Laser-target your presentation to only what they ask for and need.** Avoid doing an information dump (We are oldest . . . we have won x number of cases, for x dollar amounts), unless they specifically ask for that kind of information. "This is what I hear that you need. This is how I/we can help with this particular issue." Address each of their concerns or requirements. Then ask, "Did I miss anything?" If you did miss something, go back into discovery. Ask more questions.
- **Clarify what happens next:** "Remember, it is okay to tell me no." "What happens now?" "How shall we proceed?"

Traditional sales techniques stress overcoming objections and resistance with the intention of "always be closing." This brief overview of a nontraditional sales technique focuses on "never be closing" by building authentic trust and rapport with disarming honesty and allowing them to say no. Listen more than you talk. Finally, your role in this process is to ask questions so that you thoroughly understand. Then you can clearly present to them how you can solve each of their problems. By the time we reach the end, I always know if they are ready to move forward together or not.

Networking

LAURIE

The vast majority of my work comes from referrals from other lawyers. Someone from the general community has a friend or a family member who is or knows a lawyer. The community member may have a probate issue, but the only lawyer they know is a litigator. The litigator says, "I am not going to touch that probate matter with a 10-foot pole, but I know a lawyer who will." This referral process happens daily. It is important for lawyers to be connected with other lawyers. Young lawyers especially need to be in the minds of other attorneys. It takes a great deal of networking early on to get into that system.

I know no one is going to believe this, but I was born an introvert. Going into a social function, early in my career, I would panic: "Oh my god, I do not want to do this. I am scared. I don't like it. I feel uncomfortable going up to a stranger. 'Hi, my name is. . . .' It's the last thing I want to do." But you simply have to do it.

Recently, I was telling a story in a social situation. Midway through, I lost confidence and rushed through the end. I wasn't done, but I wanted to be done. I was holding the space, people were listening, and suddenly I got self-conscious and let the energy dissipate. The lesson for me, both socially and professionally, was to keep the energy going through the end. We are given this challenge every day we go to work, whether in court or not, whether solo or in a group; you simply have to keep the energy going. Networking takes time and energy, but there is no way around it.

If you are like me, an off the wall extrovert, networking is a party. However, like Laurie, many of the clients I coach hate networking. For them, it is not a party, it is torture. For you introverts, try doing the release of tension and vocal warm-up right before the event. You will be in a better place physically, both vocally and emotionally, if your energy is flowing and you are ready to go.

With my networking-reluctant clients, I share role-playing exercises. We practice together the chitchat of a networking function. We start by creating questions that you can have at the ready. When spontaneity and courage fail you, rely on other people's love of talking about themselves and have your stock questions ready. You do have to start by saying, "Hi. I am _____." Sorry, Laurie, there is really no way around that unless you want to be wall dressing all night. Practice that . . . no, seriously, practice saying your name out loud, supported by breath. Say your name with pride. Practice asking your questions. You practice openings/closings and you practice voir dire, so why would you not practice chitchat? Ask a trusted friend, colleague, or family member to role-play with you.

Think of questions that tap into an excitement or happiness factor. When people talk about what excites them or what they love, their dopamine levels go up. They attribute that feel good sensation to you—what a cool person you are![37]

Possible Opening Questions
- What is your area of law? (Pretty obvious but a place to start)
- How were you drawn (or inspired) to that?
- What are you most passionate about in your practice?
- What do you find most rewarding about that?
- What are you involved in that is exciting for you right now?

Hobbies and families are also great get-to-know-you topics. The great news for networking introverts is that most people love to talk about themselves. Get them talking, smile, and nod in response, and they will think you are the best conversationalist they met all night.

Improvisation is a great training tool for networking and for many other legal activities. What is court, after all, but one large improvisation? It is very popular right now, and most larger cities will have improv troupes or classes (check out Chicago's Second City, the Groundlings, or Improv Olympics). The skills that you can learn are transformative—even if at first glance it feels like a mortifying idea. There is a process to improv—learning to say "yes and . . . ." It is taking in everything that is tossed to you, responding in a positive way and tossing the energy back with a new idea. The more experience you gain, the more comfortable and confident you become with thinking on your feet, rolling with whatever is tossed your way, and collaborating with joy.

Face-to-face networking happens in all kinds of ways. There are organizations and groups that meet regularly for the sole purposes of networking. Some meet weekly, and some meet monthly. There are also nonprofit boards, Chambers of Commerce, BNI, Gold Star, Bold, and countless others. Some cost, some don't. If you are on your own, you should make time to attend at least one networking event weekly. The rationale is to nurture relationships and get to know people so that you can refer them to your network and they can refer you to theirs. Think of each person in a networking group not as one potential client but their entire group of friends and associates as potential clients. Lead with how you can be of service. Give them value, information, and support, and they will return the favor. And have a great Sixty-Second Pitch at the ready.

Perfecting Your Sixty-Second Pitch
One of the primary activities at many networking meetings is the Sixty-Second Pitch, also called the elevator pitch, sales pitch, or introduction.

Everyone gets thirty to sixty seconds to introduce themselves and share their work passions and the problems they solve. The point is to generate enough interest in your business that someone will ask for a coffee or a phone chat to find out more, either for themselves or for someone they know.

In the last four years, I have heard hundreds of Sixty-Second Pitches. Many of them don't communicate confidence, enthusiasm, or clarity. It is as if the speakers forgot to bring their personalities with them. They are too self-conscious to have fun or be passionate or even clear. Let me spend a few minutes talking about how to write, practice, and perform an engaging pitch.

What you say and *how* you say it are both crucial to the perfect Sixty-Second Pitch. However, most of us focus on *what* and hope that *how* takes care of itself. Truth be told, your audience will remember the *how* of your pitch long after they have forgotten the content. They will certainly remember how you made them *feel*. We all want to appear spontaneous. Effective spontaneity, however, can only come after preparation and practice. Let's break it down.

What elements should your Sixty-Second Pitch contain? (Your pitch does not have to include all; use it as a guideline only.)
- Your name
- The name of your firm and/or specialty
- What is the problem you solve?
- How have people benefited or will benefit from this?
- A specific example or story
- What is unique about your practice?
- What kind of client are you looking for?
- Conclusion: can be a summary, restating name and position. An inspiring quote can be added, or you can ask a compelling question, "Are you ready to . . . ?

Sometimes I save the name of my company until the end after I reiterate my name. And sometimes, right after my name, I ask a pointed question, using a possible emotional pain point for the listener. "Have you ever worried about . . . , lost sleep over . . . , witnessed a loved-one . . . "

This is followed by a statement of what you offer that can solve the problem. I try to tell a short story about someone I helped so that it feels specific and real. Audiences love stories. If I have a really good story, I might even open with that. The ending needs just as much attention, energy, and clarity as does the beginning. Many people stop before they actually finish, allowing energy and clarity to trail away.

Possible Verbiage for Your Sixty-Second Pitch
In celebrating your strengths, use some of the following words:

- Adept at . . .
- Proficient in . . .
- Accomplished . . .
- Dexterity . . .
- Expertise in . . .
- Savvy . . .

Communicating a sense of purpose, particularly if you are fund raising or advocating:

- Because . . .
- On behalf of . . .
- I owe it to . . .
- I'm inspired by . . .
- I want to inspire...
- I believe . . .

To appeal to the personal emotional needs of potential clients.

- Frustrated
- Concerned
- Disappointed
- Losing sleep

Reflective Journal

Write out your Sixty-Second Pitch in the Reflective Journal:

_____

_____

_____

_____

_____

(Continued)

Exercises: Practicing your Sixty-Second Pitch

Video #9: Full Vocal Warm-up
(Access the video at www.myvocalauthority.com/hervoiceinlaw.
Enter the access code: HerVoiceinLaw1212.)

Warm-up
- Release of habitual tension for ease
- Natural alignment, grounded and centered for presence
- Feet, knees
- Deep central breathing for power
- Space for resonance
- Pitch range for expressivity

Process for Practice
- Read through, breathing at each punctuation.
- Tongue-speak: say one sentence at a time in tongue-speak and say it again with tongue in its normal place. Work through the whole speech in this way.
- Bite the peach: to lift soft palate and feel a bigger space in the mouth.
- Do a read-through with attention to vowels. Relish the vowels; make a large space for each one.
- Point on the last word: gesture with a fully extended arm and point *on* the last word of each sentence. This is a practice technique; you won't do this in performance.
- Build a list up the wall. Start at the bottom of the wall near the floor and physicalize how the list grows up the wall. This is a practice technique, not for performance, to get volume and pitch build to happen naturally.
- Circle the nouns and physicalize each as you read the entire speech.
- Make words sound like what they mean. Words that describe problems should sound like problems. Solution words should sound triumphant. Be a little dramatic here—it is okay.
- What are you doing with your hands? (Review Chapter 4.) Less is more. Body language should augment the message, not detract from it. Watch a video of yourself to assess your gesture effectiveness.
- Perform for a friend or colleague and ask for feedback.

Tips for Better Sixty-Second Pitch Performances
- Warm up before the event.
- As others are speaking before your turn, begin slow, deep breathing.
- Make sure your words are clear and strong
- Keep your name and the name of your firm hyper clear.
- Make eye contact. One person–one thought.
- Don't fall off energy, volume, and clarity at the ends of sentences.
- Use pitch, rate, and volume variety.
- Have fun; let your authentic personality shine through!

When It Is Your Turn to Speak, Stand
- Find your feet.
- Soften your knees.
- Breathe.
- Make space in your mouth.
- Speak with passion, from your heart.

If you network with the same group frequently, you might want to shake up your pitch by changing stories or clarifying what kind of referrals/clients you are targeting. The more specific you are about the kinds of people or businesses you are seeking, the more your network can help you. Your audience will remember *how* you say it, before they remember *what* you say. Make them feel, make them laugh, or give them information they can use.

Sidebar

Networking starts in law school. You will get future jobs and clients from people whom you knew in school and other attorneys whom you meet through the local bar associations, Inns of Court, and other legal groups. If you are a morning person, find breakfast meetings that network. If you are not a morning person or if you want to be with your family in the mornings and evenings, find lunch or evening groups. Always have at least one legal network and one nonlegal network that offer you monthly contact. You can change networks over the years as your interests change. In those networking groups, be more than a member; be an officer. Officers get to know more people within the groups. As an officer, you will more than likely get introduced at each meeting because you will have some type of announcement or report.

—Beverly Atteberry, Attorney

When I speak to young women entering the profession, I recommend that they find allies and mentors. It is the best training you can have—seeing good attorneys in action. I would beg to work on cases of senior associates, just so I could go to every deposition or hearing and watch them. Whether they're in your office or not, shadow someone in your area of interest. If you want to do family law, medical malpractice, product liability, or corporate law, have someone show you the ropes. Experienced women lawyers are very eager to help younger lawyers. I frequently offer to co-counsel or to help someone, or I simply have them come visit with me.

More than ever, women really need to help other women. There's been a sea change lately in that. And I do think it's going to make a difference. But the statistics are still pretty sobering in terms of economic disparity, wage disparity, hierarchy within organizations, and leadership. So I do think that women need to be very supportive of and encouraging to each other by offering opportunities. The more we can do to lend a hand to each other, the more fulfilling it will be for all of us. It will also serve our clients well, whoever we're trying to help, just knowing we have those resources and networks. If we all devote a little time, it will come back to each of us twofold, threefold, fourfold.

—Lisa Riggs, Attorney

Collaborating in a Group

LAURIE

Many lawyers work with other lawyers. If you are in a firm, there may be other lawyers assigned to the case. If you are a solo practitioner, it is not unusual to co-counsel with other lawyers or use consultants. When you are opposing counsel, on opposite sides of the case, you are still expected to collaborate. The court expects you to put a scheduling order together and to conduct a pretrial conference together. There are certain situations, even though you are opponents, where you have to work together. It is important to maintain civility and professionalism.

I just came from a meeting with other lawyers who are working on the same case with multiple clients. We, as lawyers on the same team, need to be on the same page. Dealing with oversized egos can be tricky. Lawyers are used to being the "smartest person in the room." It can go badly if everyone is the smartest person in the room. It is even more challenging for women who tend to defer. In a group of professionals, historically, women talk the least. Women need to amplify each other's voices.

Laurie brings up a good point about allies and women amplifying other women's voices, as does Lisa in the Sidebar above. Many of the attorneys I interviewed mentioned the importance of women helping and supporting other women. Shena Burgess shared, "Women drawn to the law are competitive by nature. But I see a shift taking place. Women are more intentional to help other women by serving as sounding boards, moral support, and mentors."

Collaborations with other attorneys, as Laurie said above, can be tricky given the egos that are often involved. Some people seem effort-lessly good at it. Many people lose sleep at the thought. What is it that makes it a sticky process? Fear of failure? Fear of looking weak? Fear of letting your client down? Probably all of the above. "I need what I need, you need what you need. How do we bring those together so that we both get what we need?" Is that even possible? In my thirties, I wanted to understand collaboration, get along with others, and have well-adjusted social interactions. I wasn't doing it well. It caused a good bit of angst, and I wanted to get better at it. I went back to school to get an MA in Guidance and Counseling. Group Dynamics class was hard on me, and, as a result, it had a profound effect on how I viewed the collaborative process. I now understand the developmental phases of a group and the roles that different people play within a group. I know that I was/ am a mediator who tries to bring opposing sides together—not a bad role. I am actually kind of proud of that. But all this understanding and vocabulary didn't help me find a peaceful and satisfying way to exist within groups generally, I still found them to be pretty stressful. Why do I react as I do, often in ways that are counterproductive to my needs and interests? Why do other people behave as they do in collaborative situations? In this search, I discovered Transactional Analysis followed by Nonviolent Communication. A process began to take shape for me.

Out of my own need to understand and to answer the needs of my clients, I have blended two communication models together to form a study in Voicing Difficult Conversations, which has been valuable to my clients.

Transactional Analysis, developed by Eric Berne,[38] provides a vocab-ulary to describe what happens in the interactions between people. Granted that what is presented below is an oversimplification of a psy-chotherapeutic model, but it can provide a construct for understanding why people behave as they do in collaborative situations.

Each of us carries inside of us three ego states:

- Critical Parent: Judgmental, often harshly so. That part of us that uses language like, "You always . . . ," "You never . . . ," "You shouldn't . . . ," "Don't do that."
- Adult: Rational, evaluates, validates, and processes; speaks the language of questions.
- The Whiney Child: whose response often takes the form of "That's not fair." "It's always my fault."

Each of us carries all three of these ego states into every social interac-tion. One comes forward to lead or direct our interaction, often without conscious choice. It is the interface of my current ego state and the current ego states of others with whom I interact that affects behavior, language, and the social or professional outcome.

I like my adult best. She is grounded, she breathes deeply, and she stands easily tall. She is confident and strong without ever being strident or shrill. My critical parent is shrill and strident. When I get triggered, usually by what I perceive as stupidity, I take on that tone and begin speaking in what my husband calls "my teacher tone." However, if someone comes at me from their critical parent, I go to my child and get whiney; I hate to be scolded. Yet I know that true communication can take place only if both parties are in their adult.

So I have two tasks. If I am triggered, how do I get back to my adult? If the other person is triggered, how can I help her get back to her adult? The first is definitely within my control. I must be aware when my emotional world is changing. I may be conscious that my breathing has gotten high, fast, or shallow, or my face has flushed, or my lips pursed. Hopefully, I catch it before my words or behavior visibly change. I breathe more slowly and deeply. I relax my shoulders; I relax my jaw. I ask myself a couple of questions: What are you reacting to and why? And then I buy time by asking questions out loud: "Can you help me understand this?" "I am not sure I am following; can you give us more details?" "How did you arrive at this conclusion?" I continue to breathe deeply. To keep my voice from being shrill or whiney, I think "space." If I am making space in my mouth, my chances of getting shrill are minimized.

At other times I may be aware that someone else in the group has been triggered. I can tell by their words, their body language, their facial expression, and their breath. I ask them questions: "Tell me more about that? I need to get a clearer picture; can you give me more details?" "What are the possible rewards or advantages to this plan?" "What could be the possible unintended consequences?" If we can all find our way to our adults, we can begin to communicate.

From there, I turn to the nonviolent communication model developed by Marshall Rosenberg.[39] There are workbooks on this model and practice groups all around the world. I will describe it briefly, and hopefully, I will whet your appetite enough to go to the original source.

The model starts with an **observation** without judgment. For example; "I notice . . . ," "I see . . . ," "I observed that . . . ," "You were late three times this week," "You looked at your cell phone five times during the meeting," "You interrupted me four times." You offer no value judgment or show any sarcasm or overt irritation—just a statement of the observable facts.

The second step is a statement of **feeling**: "I feel angry." "I feel frustrated." "I feel disappointed." A feelings inventory is available online at https://www.cnvc.org/training/resource/feelings-inventory to help you find the accurate feeling word. Just state the feeling as rational fact. Expressing feelings in this way does not weaken you; rather, it makes you human. The other person is likely to drop, or at least lessen, his defenses against you.

Sample Feeling Words
- Feelings when needs are being met: affectionate, confident, engaged, excited, grateful, hopeful, joyful
- Feelings when needs are not being met: annoyed, angry, disgusted, uneasy, detached, tense, embarrassed, tired, sad, vulnerable, scared, frustrated, disappointed

Sample Feeling Statements
- I feel dismissed when you don't respond to my ideas.
- I feel displaced, with all this new technology in the office.
- I feel angry when you cut me off before the end of my presentation.
- I felt belittled when I heard you say "that's a girl thing."

The third step is connecting a feeling with a **need**. "I feel . . . because I need. . . ."

Sample needs words include autonomy, empathy, honesty, meaning, safety, respect, community, contribution, authenticity, transparency, acceptance, support, to be valued, mutuality, equity, and compassion.

Sample Needs Statements
- I feel frustrated when these errors occur because I need our firm to project a professional image.
- I feel disappointed when you correct me in public because I need mutual respect.

If we express our needs, they have a better chance of getting met.

There is a needs inventory online at https://www.cnvc.org/training /resource/needs-inventory.

The fourth and final step in the nonviolent communication model is a **request**. Say what you would like rather than what you do not want. "Would you be willing to . . . " "Can I ask that . . . " Use positive concrete action language when making requests.

We often know ahead of time when a significant conversation needs to happen. I think through the model, I try on phrases to determine which terminology most accurately reflects what I see, how I feel, what I need, and what my desired outcome would be. The more I think through the process before I am in the heat of an important conversation, the more likely I am to get the results I want.

If someone else in the collaborative group is triggered, you can use the model to help get them back to their adult. By asking questions you can lead them to making an observation. "What is it that you saw, experienced, or witnessed?" Probe for the details. "How do you feel about that?" Help them find the right feeling word. "What do you need right now?" "If you could request an action or a response, what would it be?" Just as the process works when *you* have an issue; it can also work when *someone else* has an issue, and you are in a position to facilitate their thought process. Of course, it is all, finally, an improvisation. Like most legal interactions, the behavior and language of the other person are variables you cannot control. You can, however, control yourself and, at the very least, lay the groundwork for a productive, compassionate conversation.

Presenting in Public

Apart from openings and closings, an attorney has numerous opportunities to speak in public—nonprofit boards where attorneys can bring a lot of value, fundraising, advocacy, networking, or teaching seminars. How you represent yourself in those public presentations is a networking calling card. I have gotten more paying business as a result of people hearing me speak than any other single source. So it behooves you to be the best speaker and presenter you can be in those situations.

I recently coached an attorney client who gave a speech at her best friend's investiture as a judge. The issues we worked on were the same ones I see almost universally. She brought in a beautifully written tribute. However, when she spoke it out loud, she went too fast, didn't connect to breath, didn't honor the key words, and fell off at the ends of phrases. She has a wonderful personality, but she wasn't bringing it to her speech. She was just reading words rather than sharing thoughts, stories, love, and respect for her dear friend's accomplishments. The idea is to make the audience feel what you feel, see what you see, and share your authentic self with them. This is no small task, I know. How do you make a written speech sound like you are speaking impromptu, off the cuff, with perfectly formed and organized thoughts and sentences? It is a process and, no matter how good you get at it, it is still a process. If you try to shortcut any steps, your final performance will be diminished. As I outline here the process for you to follow, you will see references to previous chapters.

I am going to assume that you know how to structure a good speech: an introduction that arouses interest and buy in, points of information, stories that illustrate points, and a conclusion. Before we start the preparation process, another quick word about the importance of breath. The largest section in Chapter 1 is about breath for speech. Connecting to a deep central breath is something that won't be accomplished without daily practice and repetition. I have mentioned this rule of thumb previously, but it bears repeating. You need to breathe every seven to nine words. If the audience is going to take in what you are saying and follow your thoughts, they need you to breathe every seven to nine words. That translates to the fact that phrases and clauses need to be seven to nine words in length. You don't need to breathe at each comma in a list, for example, apples, oranges, bananas. But when a comma separates a clause, breathe; after a semicolon, breathe; at a period, exclamation point, or question mark, breathe. Read aloud what you have written to make sure the phrases are not overlong. For a few words, you need a small breath; for a medium-length phrase, you need a medium breath; for big emotions, high-volume, or more words, you need a big breath.

Preparing Your Presentation
- Warm up. Go back to Chapter 1. Tune your instrument and prepare your voice and body for the work. Video #9 has the full vocal warm-up.
- Read through the speech, breathing at punctuation. Don't worry about interpretation yet or how you're going to say it. Just read and breathe. Your body is memorizing where the breaths go.
- Read it through again, focusing on space for vowels. Long vowels need more space and time than short vowels. Relish the vowels; taste them! If you want to move a little with this, you can review the vowel dance.
- Read it one more time, at a number 2 volume level, and make each consonant snap. Make those plosives p, b, t, d, k, g explode. Let the fricatives s, z, ch, sh, f, v linger and hiss.
- You need a read-through for jaw and tongue release. I recommend first doing the acupressure on the jaw hinge as described in Chapter 1. Then tongue-speak: one sentence with tongue hanging out, followed by keeping the tongue in its regular place. Go back and forth throughout. Be easy, have fun. It is silly—but embrace the silly!
- If you found biting the peach helpful to lift the soft palate, try a read-through, refreshing the sensation of biting the peach at each new breath. Keep this easy at effort level two or three. It is just to open easy space in the back of the mouth.
- Circle each noun. Then read it through, physicalizing as you say the noun. The physicalizing can be extravagant, abstract, or dance-like, or it can be subtle, whichever style you are comfortable with. Notice what happens to the word when you physicalize it—it may lift, lengthen, or carry more emotion or be clearer. Then read it through again, letting the nouns be whatever they want to be.

- Circle the action verbs. Read the speech again, this time physical-izing the verbs.
- Then read it again and see if the verbs have a bit more life and interest.
- Point on the last word of each sentence, with energized finger and arm, as you read through the speech. As I stated in earlier in this chapter, in "Perfecting Your Sixty-Second Pitch," this is not a per-formance technique. Rather, it is a rehearsal strategy for bringing the end of sentences up and out to the audience.
- Find authentic pitch variety and inflection. You can do this using the exercises from Chapter 2:
  ◦ One to Ten Shoot for the Middle
  ◦ Master Thespian
  ◦ Pitch Absurd

  Read the entire speech in one of these three exercises. Then just release the speech and read it, enjoy it, and let the inflection go where it wants to. It should now begin to sound like your authen-tic storytelling style and not a talking head or speaker-bot.
- Make a video of your speech. Listen for clarity of words, phrases, and forward energy at ends of sentences. Does your body lan-guage support the message?
- Bring your heart. What are the words you want the audience to really feel? Circle those words. Say each one separately several times. Connect that word to your center and your breath. What does this word mean to you? What picture do you see when you say that word? What do you want the audience to feel when they hear that word? Say it until you have a feeling of what the word means to you in your center. Then put it back in the sentence it came from.
- Find the arc of the story. Your speech has variety built into it, and now you need to find and explore those options. There is a roadmap of sorts—first it starts here, then it moves to here, then to here, and finally to the big finish. You provide the audience with the signs that make the map clear. What is your goal in sec-tion one? To make them feel welcome? Then with your tone and body language, welcome them as if you were opening the door and greeting them warmly into your home. Is the second section to make them laugh? How does your tone and body language change in order to do that? Do you want to warn them, to scare them, to motivate them to act? Use verb images that inspire your voice and body to reflect the image of the verb. Review the section "Inspiring Imagination with Action Verbs" in Chapter 3.

- Perform your speech for family, friends, or colleagues and ask for their feedback. The more you perform for an audience, the better your final performance will be.

> ## LAURIE
>
> I'd like to interject one last nontrial-speaking situation. Lawyers do a lot of panels. Continuing Legal Education organizers don't want to pick just one person to speak on a topic; instead, they assemble a panel. Then you are dealing with group dynamics in front of an audience. I have never seen it work really well. But we keep doing it. Seated with a table in front of you, you will find it hard to keep enthused. If I have to sit, give me a stool and don't put a table in front of me to block the flow of energy. If you have no say in the physical setup, at least you can sit forward, so the energy doesn't dissipate into the floor. You still need to extend your energy out to the audience. Don't dull yourself down to match the panel. Don't be embarrassed to be animated, passionate, and enthused.

Pretrial Work

Negotiating

My negotiations guru, Ed Brodow, lays out an entire process for a winning negotiation technique in his book *Negotiation Boot Camp*.[40] He speaks of the Confidence Mystique, "If you give signals that you are in charge, that you know what you are doing, you are less likely to be victimized. . . . People bow to confidence. What is behind the self-assuredness is secondary to the impression it makes." In terms of our process, we can look at the principles of power without press and strategies for owning the room; both feed into your Confidence Mystique.

- Are you connected to deep central breath?
- Are you grounded and centered?
- Are you carrying yourself in a natural alignment: head floating up as your face is forward, chin parallel to the floor?
- Are your eyes alive and sparkling? This says, "I am going to enjoy this."
- Enter and shake hands with each person. If you don't know them, introduce yourself in your strong but friendly voice. Upon entering, go around the table and introduce yourself to each person. If you are seated when others come in, stand and extend your hand. Make it your party; it is your job to make everyone feel welcome, even if you are not on your home turf. Start building disarming trust and rapport.

- Don't let yourself be triggered. Don't take anything personally. Stay connected to your breath. Check in with your shoulders. Use your body language intentionally.

Through the negotiations, listen more than you talk. Ed suggests we listen 70 percent of the time and talk the other 30 percent. Ask questions, gather information.

Ed teaches a fabulous negotiating body language technique called the Flinch. You use it when the opposition throws out a figure or proposes an idea or solution in the negotiation that is not to your liking. It is a grimace, a sound, a wince—whatever response is authentic to you. The Flinch sends a hidden message, "Your behavior is so outrageous, your request is so ridiculous that it doesn't even deserve a response, except to dismiss it completely." It is a body language signal that acts on a subconscious level. The impact of the Flinch is emotional and nonverbal. Your negotiation partner/opponent experiences a tight sensation in the pit of the stomach, accompanied by the thought, "Obviously my request was too high."[41]

If you really want to master the art of negotiation, I highly recommend a deep dive into the Negotiation Boot Camp.

Sidebar

Like most lawyers, a lot of my time is spent negotiating. That was true when I was litigating and trying cases, and it is true now. I have a lot of experience negotiating a host of issues in the context of litigating and trying cases—from legal hold and discovery issues to the resolution of cases. But now, rather than negotiating in the context of litigation, most of my negotiations involve terms, particularly privacy and security terms, in my clients' agreements with their customers and vendors.

I was once brought in to resolve a high-stakes litigation matter that a silk-stocking law firm was handling for one of my clients. Because the attorney who was representing my client in the litigation matter had a very antagonistic relationship with the plaintiff's attorney, he was getting nowhere in settlement negotiations. I was able to resolve that matter for an amount that was many millions of dollars less than my client's litigation counsel had told the client was possible. I invested a lot of time at the beginning of my involvement in that matter just listening and building a relationship with opposing counsel and his client.

In negotiations, I seek to control the agenda. And I always come well prepared. As with every aspect of practicing law, thorough preparation is critical. It is important to give a lot of thought to your client's needs and desires, as well as your clients options in the event an agreement is not reached. I think it is important to stay calm – no matter what your opponent is doing. I have had opposing lawyers literally screaming at me in the midst of negotiations. Remaining calm has served me and my clients well in the context of negotiations and otherwise.

—Laura Clark Fey, Attorney

Little did I know when I did the negotiations competition during my first year of law school (I won the competition with my partner Gwen Clegg) that it would control my career. Negotiations occur every day in the practice of law. In my criminal practice, I negotiate with the prosecutors on behalf of my client to work out the best deal. In civil law, there are negotiations between attorneys to work out settlement agreements. There have been times when we have gone into mediations that failed. But the attorneys were able to negotiate a settlement after the fact. I've been pretty lucky that I have not had any negotiations that have gone poorly. I did have a criminal case where I had hired an expert and was awaiting a result of the evaluation on my client. I told the prosecutor that if the result came back as battered women syndrome, I believed that the jury would acquit my client, so we would offer ten years to manslaughter, one down from murder in the first degree (life/life without parole) if he agreed to it before I got my results. We were able to get my client from the jail that day to plead her. The report was not favorable to my client, so it was a huge win.

    I approach negotiations from a neutral position, whether it be civil or criminal. When attorneys get too emotional during this part of the case, people put their guard up and communication fails. You can advocate for your client with zeal without taking a personal stake in it. The passion is for the jury, not negotiations. I try to ask questions from the other side to have them explain their offer or counteroffer to me. I once told a prosecutor that he couldn't verbally justify a recommendation to me because it sounded like he didn't have a good reason for it. If I cast doubt in this way, I can generally get a better deal. On the flip side, you have to be able to explain why your offer is just and works to satisfy all parties.

    I walk into the negotiations already knowing what my client is willing to do and not do. That way the negotiation is fluid and ongoing. When you have to stop the dialogue each time to check on every issue, it gets tedious and the negotiations will break down. Negotiations occur when you have read the discovery, know the law, and are in a position to get the best result for your client.

—Shena Burgess, Attorney

In my practice, not much time is spent negotiating in the traditional sense. I negotiate when I'm trying to settle a case, and that is often a traditional-type negotiation, sometimes involving a paid mediator. Negotiating usually takes up a small fraction of the time spent investigating, developing, and pursuing the case. Other times I negotiate with opposing counsel on general discovery, scheduling, and general matters on the case.

Most challenging for me is being a strong advocate for my client, while weighing the balancing of conceding certain matters in order to keep the case moving and getting concessions in return. In settlement negotiations, it is a challenge to gauge what is the most appropriate opening settlement offer. I work really hard to pursue only meritorious cases, but every case has its risks. Factoring the risk of an unsatisfactory result into the evaluation of a fair result for the client is always difficult, and every case is different.

My approach in all cases is to be as factual and straightforward as possible. I like to put all information on the table and discuss it openly and honestly. If my case has problems, I like to address them and factor that into my proposals and discussions. I don't really try to hide the ball—I try to deal with everything up front. I try to be reasonable when negotiating over discovery or scheduling issues because I sometimes need concessions in return, and I want to save the fights for issues that really do matter.

—Lisa Riggs, Attorney

Preparing Clients for Deposition and Trial

LAURIE

It is a given that 90 percent of clients or witnesses are going to be terrified. Many people are afraid to speak in public anyway; then you stick them in this big scary legal situation. Even if they are telling the truth, they are freaked out! You can spend days preparing them, but it is still not the real thing, and so you don't know how they are going to react.

I coach on body language, how to sit in the chair, what to do with one's hands and where to look, and of course we role-play questions and answers. The biggest obstacle to a good deposition or trial performance is fear, anxiety, and emotions that may be triggered when recounting traumatic events. The most helpful thing I do is focus on how my clients are breathing. In one case, I brought a client off the ceiling and back to herself through a meditation–style breath exercise. We couldn't progress while she was triggered. Simple breath work allowed us to move forward.

I had another client who I knew was not going to do well with the jury. She conveyed an impression that was not going to help the case. I noticed that in the deposition she came across as whiney. The problem wasn't so much what she was saying as how she was saying it, her tone. Her speech became nasal and grating. I could say "Stop that!" But that wouldn't help. It is at this point that I call in a professional help. I call Rena. She can quickly diagnose the problem and give the client a few practical tips to change that vocal behavior.

In my experience, the witnesses who aren't visibly nervous are professional witnesses. But I prepare them as well, as much as they will let me. The expert witness who is too glib or suave is not found to be believable by the jury. Juries give lay witnesses who are nervous or anxious a lot of slack.

Whether I am coaching actors or witnesses, I start with the releasing habitual tension warm-up. You can't appear relaxed if you are carrying your habitual set of tensions with you. I talk about feeling grounded and centered and how to achieve that feeling through deep central breathing. I typically start with the "slower, deeper, quieter, calmer exercise" (Chapter 3). I do it with them until I see that they have truly relaxed. I call attention to how they feel and reassure them that when they feel emotionally triggered, going back to the breath will help them ground and center. I may also teach them the 4–7–8 breath. I let them practice both breath exercises by themselves so they will learn how to do it on their own, without me present.

I share the following checklist of behaviors.

- Sit straight but relaxed in the chair, long back of neck and shoulders relaxed and down. If seated in a swivel chair, don't swivel.
- Keeps hands still in the lap or resting on the arms of the chair. Don't fiddle or fuss.
- Keep the shaking foot or leg still. Many people exhibit this nervous habit when they are under pressure. Stretching and shaking prior to the testimony can provide some relief. Noticing the behavior and taking a deep breath can help still the distraction.
- Chin parallel to the floor communicates easy confidence. An elevated chin looks cocky or arrogant; a tucked or retracted chin looks guilty or insecure.
- The dos and don'ts of eye contact. If clients have trouble making eye contact, practice it with them. Should they look at the jury? Should they look at you? Whichever your preference, practice it with them. The more practice, the better chance the behavior will stick under pressure.
- Pause to breathe before responding to a question.
- Answer the question honestly and simply. Don't volunteer more than is asked.

Praise when they do well. Don't ever say, "Wrong!" Empower, don't demean. No one ever remains relaxed and confident when they are afraid of doing it wrong. When I coached award-winning actors in competitions, I reminded them of key points and touchstones even as they walked on stage. Always in reassuring ways, tell them, "You got this. You can do this. Breath is your life line."

Most of this you already know. The points that I usually reinforce, even with attorneys who are very good at this, is the power of repetition. Repeat breath exercises, applying breath as a focus during role playing and improvisation. Be creative in how you structure practice runs. Actors spend hours and hours repeating lines and movement so that they will appear totally spontaneous, natural, and authentic. It simply takes time to learn unfamiliar behaviors and speech patterns so that they can be reproduced under the pressure of a deposition or trial.

Sidebar

Depositions or examinations are not a conversation, and it's not really about the story itself. It is about making sure the facts match up with how your legal requirements are set out.

As far as witness prep goes for deposition, I try to walk through all possibilities with the client. I tell the client, first and foremost, only answer the question that is asked of you. Do not offer up information. Don't allow the opposing attorney to get a rise out of you or make you emotional. Do not look to me before answering a question because it will look like you want me to indicate how you should answer. Don't take anything like Xanax or alcohol to ease your nerves because we won't be able to take the deposition as it could impair your ability to participate.

We prepare our clients for the deposition partly because the client is coming from a place of emotion and the attorney is coming from a technical place. We all say things we don't mean when we are emotional. This tendency can be especially damaging in a deposition or at trial when your every word is dissected. So, we need to walk through what clients want to say and make sure that they use the words that convey the story accurately. We also need to make sure that the client is emotionally prepared to do this. In that vein, I had the surviving spouse of a woman who died of a heart attack on her living room floor because the ambulance took almost an hour to get there. During this time, my client called 911 several times, while watching the firemen do chest compressions on his wife (for about 45 minutes) in order to try to save her. The calls were fraught with emotion and were terrible to hear. Opposing counsel chose to go through the phone calls, line by line, and stop to question my client about each statement that he made to the 911 operator. My client kept it together beautifully. Once the deposition was over and opposing counsel had left the room, my client began to sob. He had held his emotions at bay until he absolutely couldn't anymore. He had just relived the worst moment of his life. Line by line. We ultimately got a good settlement for him, and he was able to get closure on what happened. I truly believe that he could have singlehandedly wrecked his case if he had let emotion take over.

—Kathleen Pence, Attorney

In preparing witnesses for trial or to testify for a hearing, I sit down with them in person and discuss if they want to testify. They have an absolute right not to under the Fifth Amendment. We discuss the pros and cons of their testimony; and then I have them practice answering direct questions so that they can get a feel for, and a rhythm of, how the questions go. I then will bring in another attorney to cross examine them. I bring in an outside counsel because he or she does not know the person. Outside counsel has not bonded with the client. This attorney can then go after the client on cross to see how they hold up. It is after that experience that my client and I can make the decision on whether or not to testify.

The rules that I tell my clients who are testifying are these:

1. *Always tell the truth. I can deal with any truth no matter how bad the fact is. If you lie, then you have set off a hand grenade in the trial that will explode, usually when I'm standing on it.*
2. *Listen carefully to each question. If you don't understand it, ask that it be repeated or rephrased.*
3. *Look at the jury when you are answering the question. The jury is the judge of the facts; the jurors are the ones who have to understand your story.*
4. *Only answer what the question asks. If I want more information, I will ask another question. If the other party only gets half the story, I get another opportunity to fill it in. Don't advocate; just be a witness.*
5. *Never volunteer information to be helpful. It is never helpful.*
6. *Never speculate, guess, or tell what probably happened. If you don't remember, say so.*
7. *Only testify to what you know, not what someone else has told you.*
8. *Always review your previous statements.*
9. *If you are emotional, that is okay; you are human.*
10. *Be yourself; tell your story truthfully.*

I tell my clients from the beginning to always tell the truth. Their job is not to win the case but to be authentic and genuine.

—Shena Burgess, Attorney

Using Voice in Depositions

> ### LAURIE
>
> Depositions are for information gathering. One area in which women excel natu-
> rally, whether it is genetic or cultural, is listening. Most women are good listeners.
> When witnesses feel they are really being listened to, they are inclined to say
> more. I get more information that way. I tend to lead with listening. In some depo-
> sitions, that may be all I do. In other depositions, I will lead with empathetic lis-
> tener, get all the information I need, and then flip to a more aggressive approach.

How does one listen empathetically? What happens in the voice and
body that builds trust and rapport? You want your body to be open and
your voice to be warm. Make time and space for a warm-up, starting
with release of habitual tension. You can't pretend to be welcoming and
attentive if you are stressed or tense. Use the warm-up in Chapter 1 or
create one of your own. It should include the major body parts and con-
sist of shaking, stretching, and deep breathing.

Warm up your voice as well. A cold voice can sound brittle and harsh
or thin and creaky. A vocal warm-up can be as simple as humming up
and down your pitch range, releasing your jaw and tongue, and yawning
easily with big space in your mouth. The Tai Chi or Archer exercises
get the voice easily motoring. Also do something to get the articulators
going. Tune your instrument before you walk into the room.

Behaviors That Communicate Empathetic Listening and Build Trust and Rapport

- Offer a beverage and indicate where the restrooms are.
- Sit tall in your chair and lean forward slightly.
- Face the witness straight on.
- Make eye contact in an easy, natural way.
- Keep chin parallel to the floor.
- Have shoulders relaxed and down.
- Relax hands on the table, or one on the table with one in your lap.
- Nod occasionally to signal "Yes, I hear you."
- Verbalize to indicate you are listening: "Uhhuh." "I see." "Tell me more about that." "Go on."
- Paraphrase their feelings, "You were angry."

Revisiting the concept of power without press might be useful here.
In a deposition, you don't want to concede power or appear weak.
This also may not be the best environment in which to appear overly

forceful or aggressive, at least not at first. Let's review power without press. You are connected to slow, deep breathing. Your shoulders are relaxed and down, your chin is parallel with the floor, your jaw is released. Your energy is deep in your body, not high in the chest. You are present, in the moment, and you are listening—not to the negative voices in your own head; but you are actively listening to the witness being deposed.

Sidebar

In a deposition, I want witnesses to feel as comfortable with me as they are with their own attorneys. So when they walk in, I introduce myself. I go over and shake their hand. If they're at my place, "Would you like something to drink? Let me show you where the bathroom is." It's very conversational. "We've been going for about an hour, would you like a break?" People drop their guard and tell me more than they intended.

But that's my job. In the courtroom, however, when we're in trial and I have an audience, the niceties are gone.

Now, if they're helpful witnesses, even if they're opposing counsel's witnesses, I'm going to start out and get all the good stuff that I need from them to make my case. When I have that done, I'm going in to, as my 15-year-old calls me, "attorney mode." We're going to be short. We're going to be to the point. "You're going to answer my question. You're going to answer how I want it, and then we're going to move on." I take control both physically, verbally.

When I have laid the groundwork to impeach them, I do it quickly. I do it on something completely solid, and that way, they're not going to challenge me on anything else. If you can impeach them the first time solidly, they're not going to mess with you on the witness stand.

I think attorneys who go into depositions very aggressively are completely off the mark. I get so much more information from witnesses because I don't have to be a jerk—not in depositions. There's no audience.

—Shena Burgess, Attorney

Hearing in Front of a Judge

LAURIE

There are two types of meetings with judges: formal and informal. Hearings or arguing a point require a more formal demeanor. However, collaborating or scheduling are less formal; you can be yourself to a greater extent.

I know we have talked about pauses and silences, but I want to reinforce the power of the pause or silence in hearings. I've watched lawyers who were winning the argument; I mean it was just within reach. If they had known when to shut up, they would have won. Often a lawyer does not listen, watch, or read the judge. When they should have stopped, they talk the judge out of that position. It is better to say too little than too much.

As you are standing outside the judge's door, take a moment before you enter. Check to see if you are grounded and centered. Find your feet, soften your knees, relax your shoulders, release your jaw, and take a deep breath. You don't want to enter literally with a "head of steam." Feel that energy alive in your center, not shooting out your ears. Walk in slowly and deliberately. Take a breath as you determine if you are going to sit or stand. Take another breath as you take in the judge's mood or receptivity to your presence. Breathe before you speak. If you give yourself a little extra space in the back of your mouth, your voice will be strong but not strident. And as Laurie points out, don't talk too fast or say too much. Don't let silence scare you into saying more than you need to.

Trial Work

> Trial preparation is very much like making taffy. You are constantly pulling at it, you're writing out what you want to say, and you're constantly revising it. You're standing up and you are saying it out loud. You are evaluating: Does this work? Is this what I want to say? No. Scratch that. You are pulling at the taffy and trying to make it into what it needs to be until you have gone through it so many times you know where your signposts are. You don't really want a memorized script because, if you lose your place, you're lost. You want signposts. You discover certain phrases you want to use; a certain picture you want to paint. Yes, it's like pulling taffy.
>
> —Kathleen Pence, Attorney

Taming Stridency

When Laurie and I were last talking about trial work, she said the first thing to address is taming stridency. I have spoken a lot about this already, but as it is the most talked about feature of women attorneys, I am going to add some information to this conversation.

As I was beta testing possible titles for this book with a group of women attorneys, I pitched the title "Overcoming Bitch Perception."

I saw smiles, nodding heads, and a couple of knowing chuckles. One woman then said confidently, "I don't mind being called a bitch; I know I am doing my job well." Although her comment drew me up short for a moment, I was grateful that she shared this point of view. It made me rethink not only the title but also how I look at stridency and power.

Stridency can be effective as a strategy, when used occasionally and with intention. It should not be a permanent delivery mode or a habit that is with you all the time. It is not useful in all situations. As a matter of fact, it can be damaging in many situations. It is not useful when winning over a jury, when coaxing a vulnerable witness, or when building trust and rapport with a client. You need vocal flexibility. You need several different voices that are authentic to you and comfortable to use.

I have had clients ask, "Isn't changing my voice inauthentic? It feels manipulative." We change our voices instinctively when we are with our children, our spouses, our parents, and our circle of best friends. We adapt behavior and voice to meet the demands of the social situation. Code shifting is what well-adjusted people do. For the attorney, developing a flexible voice is adding depth to your arsenal.

"This is just the way I sound," or "This is the voice I was born with," are statements that I hear frequently. Barring illness or accident, these statements are just not true. A habitual voice quality like stridency, nasality, mumbling, breathiness, up-speak, overly loud, or too soft are just vocal habits developed over years.

The habitually strident voice usually contains constriction in the vocal tract somewhere—tension in jaw and tongue, small tight space in the mouth—and insufficient breath. All these muscle habits create a need to push to get sound out. Couple that with the misconception that you have to be strident to be taken seriously in court, and you have the perfect storm for a harsh voice.

Tempering stridency does not mean you will go to the opposite extreme and have a weak voice. I was recently coaching a third-year law student interning for a big law firm. She is very bright and gentle in nature. She says in a high, light, almost breathy tone, "I am afraid I may not be taken seriously in court." She is the opposite of strident. As we worked, I showed her how to breathe deeply for speech, how to access support from her abdominal muscles, how to release tension in the jaw and tongue, and how to make space in her mouth. To her surprise and joy, her woman's voice emerged. Not strident, but powerful, rich, and warm. Now, of course, we did not flip a switch and she is forever cured. She will have to practice on a regular basis to retrain many years of vocal usage habits to get her powerful sound to be her default. At least now she knows it exists.

Notice that for both extremes—strident or breathy—the prescription is the same: breathe deeply, access support, release tongue and jaw, make space in the mouth. The difference is in effort level and where that effort is happening in the body. With a strident voice, too much effort is expended in jaw, tongue, throat, and chest; the sound is pressed. With the light and breathy voice, effort needs to be dialed up in breathing and accessing support from the abdominals. Using the exercises described in Chapter 1 will help either habit come to power without press.

Picking a Jury

LAURIE

Voir dire, jury selection, is a crucial part of your success, and it is a mysterious process to many lawyers. I have attended numerous training and development seminars, and I have observed the supreme interest in this topic. If five different topics are offered, 80 percent of lawyers go to voir dire. That tells me it is the area that people want to work on the most; it is also the area they are least comfortable with.

This huge task requires attention, training, and experience. It is our first opportunity to make connection with individuals in the jury pool. As much as ferreting out bias that may disqualify them, you need to connect with them. You need them to like you. How do I make this connection? How painful will it be to make this kind of connection with someone I don't know. It is hard for most people to do that.

The second and equally important task is keeping the list of questions you need to ask in your head, while you are listening and being present for each speaker. When I train lawyers in voir dire, I give them back the tools they need. Somewhere along the line, we picked up the idea that you shouldn't use notes because it is a barrier to communication. Without notes, the attorney must carry this laundry list of questions in her head. Imagine this: someone from the jury pool is talking to me, but I am focused on the list in my head, planning where do I go next. I am not truly listening.

I don't think using notes is bad. The key is how you physically use them and when. I can set them on a table. It is perfectly fine to walk to the table to get your next thought. You can't listen and get your next thought at the same time. I listen to what they are saying, until they have concluded. Then I can check my notes for where to go next. I am not going to talk to them while I am looking at my notes.

Eye contact is crucial in making that connection. Every lawyer knows you should make eye contact with the jury; it is a given. But many don't maintain eye contact long enough. I recommend that you hold the contact until the jurors look away. And then maybe a second longer. Voir dire is really an intimate conversation with a complete stranger.

The best way to get better at voir dire is to watch other people do it. I become a better lawyer by watching someone else do it. I take every opportunity to watch or assist by taking notes for a colleague. If someone asks me, I am there.

In my firm, we have at least two people watching and taking notes. It is my job to make that intimate connection. If I am holding eye contact with a potential juror and someone else in the jury pool displays negative body language, I can't turn away and look, I have violated the trust of connection. I don't take notes in voir dire. Someone else needs to do that.

Another hard lesson I have learned is to "believe what they are saying." A potential juror told me her hobby was sleeping. Guess what she did throughout the trial? Another told me, "I march to my own drummer." The verdict was 11 to 1. And guess who the 1 was? Trust your gut. The gifts of aging and experience are stronger and more accurate intuitive responses. You become more capable of reading the small things. The experienced lawyer trusts her gut.

In voir dire, it is especially important to be aware of voice and body language. You know I am going to remind you to warm up before so that your body and voice are ready to do your best work. Check in with your alignment, make sure feet are grounded and knees are released. Shoulders are relaxed and down, chin is parallel to the floor. Don't sway, shift, or shuffle. Stay connected to breath and keep space in the back of your mouth so that your voice is warm, welcoming, and clear.

Exercise: Eye Contact

If eye contact is a challenge for you, here are two variations of an exercise that force you to maintain eye contact for the duration of the potential juror's answer. Do this with a focus group or in a practice session with colleagues. I referenced this exercise in Chapter 3: offer your hand to potential jurors as they answer your question. As you make eye contact, continue holding their hand until they have finished their answer. I coach the exercise partner to ask for eye contact if it is not adequately delivered.[42]

Laurie describes a different version of the exercise with a similar outcome. Hold an object between you and the juror as they talk. You listen and hold eye contact. The object could be something as simple as a water bottle. The bottle becomes a tangible bond between the two of you, as it forces you to stay focused on the speaker.

Sidebar

Voir dire is a challenging aspect of trial work because often jurors are not honest, even with themselves. I've read a lot about it; I've taken Continuing Legal Education courses. But I still find a high level of unpredictability with the process that makes me uncomfortable. I rarely try a case by myself. I mostly practice medical malpractice, and it's hard to do with one lawyer. So typically, whoever is not conducting voir dire takes copious notes. I have a written list of questions, and I practice that. I also have little notes about what I am trying to get at and what I'm trying to pull out. But I think it's hugely important to have someone else listening and watching because I may be communicating with you as a juror, and some juror down the line may be reacting, and I don't even see it. We typically have at least two lawyers and a paralegal at the trial. We want whoever is not doing the questioning to be observing closely.

Then we caucus. Usually the court will give you time to compare notes. I listen intently. Sometimes our legal team agrees; sometimes we don't. I have even had paid jury consultants who were very firm about certain things and got it totally wrong.

It's just so hard to pay attention, to get a feel for the jurors and go through the topics you need to cover. There's always that subset of wildcards. You're just not going to be right every time. And you only have three strikes. There's always going to be extra people you wish you could strike. Then there are people you're happy with who are struck by the opposition. So ultimately you get who you get.

—Lisa Riggs, Attorney

Genuinely, I have a bullshit detector that the average person doesn't have. I can spot a racist without the person even admitting to being a racist. In my next life, I might come back as a jury expert to help people pick juries. I see body language that other people can't pick up on. I hear inconsistencies. I read micro-expressions, and I will call them out. "You had a reaction to what I just said. Do you want to explore that a little further?" It's subconscious. They didn't realize that they did it, but I caught it. If they turn away from you, they're no longer leaning forward, they're not taking notes, if they refuse to make eye contact with you, you're losing your jury.

During jury selection, I need to spot who doesn't like me. If they don't like me, I don't have a chance. I need to make sure that all of my blazers have their buttons and that I don't have any runs in my hose because they're going to be paying attention to those things. My facial expressions matter. How is my hair? Is my makeup on point? Do I look tired? Do I look flustered? Do I look concerned about my case because if I'm concerned about it, the jury's going to be concerned about it as well.

—Jenny Proehl-Day, Attorney

For voir dire, I'm the hostess of a party. We're all here getting to know each other. I want to learn about you. I ask completely open-ended questions. Then in my closing, I try to use a point or fact which they used. They then feel important. "Oh my goodness, five days ago I said that. She just quoted me. She remembered that I said that." Consequently, that juror is empowered because you listened to what they said. They are more likely to advocate for you in the deliberation room.

Voir dire is not choosing jurors; it's getting rid of jurors. I'm being selective about who I don't want. I can deal with what's left. Through my questions, I will get them to look at the judge and say, "Judge, I can't be a fair and impartial juror on this case. You have to remove me." I didn't ask for them to be removed, I got the juror to do it. Because I empowered them to remove themselves.

—Shena Burgess, Attorney

Preparing Dynamic Openings/Closings

Openings and closings are aspects of trial work that you actually have control over. In theatrical terms, they are equivalent to soliloquies or arias in operas. They serve as the framing device that sets you up on your terms. You lay the groundwork for all that is to follow. It is your moment to shine. The closing is your final shot to drive it home, to give the jury their last emotionally charged image. You want to give them the tools they need to fight for you in the jury room. Nothing can be left to chance.

In Chapter 3, I laid out a process for practicing your openings and closing, to get the breath, the words, and the images in your body. In this chapter, I review that process as well as adding an overview of how to take a speech from first draft to trial-ready. It is a time-intensive process. For best results, you need to work through the process step by step, as you move from good to fabulous. You may be tempted to skip to the end and begin practicing out loud in front of focus groups or colleagues. That will just reinforce your habitual mode of delivery.

The explorative, organic work you do alone. You want to try each step outlined here with intentionality, focus, and energy. Practice like no one is watching! If your speech is long, you can break it down by section and go through all the steps below. Then move on to the next section. Be creative, and take on board what works for you. You will create your own process from the steps below or from other exercises you discovered throughout the rest of this book. It is a fluid, dynamic process.

- Warm up the body and voice. (Review video #9.)
- Read the speech through, breathing at each punctuation. You will also refine the writing as you read it out loud, connecting breath to thought.

- Read it through, enjoying vowels. Make space in our mouth for vowels; relish them. Vowels carry emotions.
- Read through at a number two volume level to articulate each consonant—first, middle, and last.
- Lift the last word of each sentence by pointing *on* the word.
- Circle the nouns. Say each noun out loud, visualize what you see when you say that word and what you want the jury to see when they hear that word. Say the word as you see the image. Now put it back in the sentence and read the entire sentence. Don't punch the noun; just see it as you say it.
- Underline the action verbs. Say each verb out loud. What is the implied action in that word? Can you make it sound like what it means? Put the verb back into the sentence and read it again. You don't need to punch the verb; just think about what it means as you say it.
- Explore inflection variety by doing one of the following previously described exercises: Pitch Absurd, Master Thespian, One to Ten Shoot for the Middle, sing it, or dance it as you speak.
- Score the speech for objectives and action verbs. In the opening paragraph, you may want to welcome, to comfort, to startle, to warn, or to evoke sympathy. (Refer to the section "Inspiring Imagination with Action Verbs" in Chapter 3 for the entire list of verbs.) Read the section with your chosen verb/objective. Mark each section with a different objective and action verb. This will help you find authentic variety in the transitions.
- Where do you want to build suspense? Will you use rate, volume, or pitch variety? Are there places for pauses/silences? (Review the exercises in Chapter 2.)
- Practice the speech through, releasing any effort you may have picked up in the explorations above.
- Make a video recording: listen for clarity or falling off at end of sentences; do you look and sound authentic? How are your gestures? If you are moving too much or not enough, review Chapter 4, which addresses gesture.
- Practice in front of a colleague or a focus group and get feedback.

Here are a few other presentation tips to keep in mind as you are preparing:

- Proper names and dates occur often in opening/closing statements. Whenever you say someone's name or give a date, say it clearly; maybe even take a tiny pause before speaking it.

- Lists often occur in openings/closings. A list has to build; it starts low (in volume, pitch, or energy) and builds to the last item.
- If you are comparing two people, actions, or ideas, which is something litigators do frequently, remember the inflection of antithesis (see Chapter 2).
- Don't stress the word "not." The stress comes on the word after "not." Don't stress the word "and." The stressed word follows the "and."
- The most important ideas or words come at the end of your sentences. Keep the ends of sentence alive and the energy moving forward toward your audience.
- Eliminate filler words. Use breath to transition from thought to thought. Don't be afraid of the silence as you breathe and gather your thoughts.
- Trust that breath is your touchstone. If you get lost, breathe; if you get thrown, breathe; as you are listening, breathe; if you sense you are racing, breathe; if you want to change direction, breathe.

LAURIE

Almost universally, lawyers talk too fast. It is the nature of our profession to beat the jury into our position with words. We think the more words the better, which is diametrically opposed to the truth. What I want to say to most lawyers I watch is, "You are going too fast and you are saying too much."

Now I understand this from a trial perspective. We only get to trial after months, sometimes years, of working with the case. We have collected so much information that our natural tendency is to give "a brain dump." We think the jury needs to know everything we know. But that is not helpful. The jurors become overwhelmed, thinking they are never going to figure this out, so they "check out." If we give them just what they need to know, they stay engaged and want to know more.

I have learned to make my opening much shorter, so that I have more time. I don't want to feel pressured to deliver massive amounts of information to the jury. I prepare much earlier than I used to. I may prepare an opening months in advance. And then, of course, I will work on it with Rena. I am more aware of pacing and pitch variety.

Dates are also problematic for juries, and lawyers love to give them—all the time. My recommendation is that once you have established the key dates, use shorthand such as "a year later" or "two weeks later."

We also know that we should use plain English rather than legalese—but we do it anyway. Even the language of the case can be simplified. For example, in a product liability case, part of a larger system failed. The name of the part was something like "cm500xz" which was repeated over and over by the attorney—a meaningless piece of gibberish which the jury stumbled over each time they heard it. The "cm500zx" was, in actuality, a safety valve that had failed! How much easier would that have been?

Projection, being heard and understood, is often an issue in the courtroom. They have large, high ceilings that were not designed with acoustics in mind. Rather, they were designed to be ceremonial representations of justice, and that directly contrasts with the need to communicate and be heard. Sometimes there are obvious visible barriers to communication. The Muskogee Court House, for example, built around 1912, was beautifully renovated a few years ago. But there are columns in the courtroom between where the attorney speaks and the jury box. How ridiculous is that! Some courtrooms have microphones, which can be helpful. But there are a lot of courtrooms that do not.

My biggest challenge in projecting is the configuration of many courtrooms. If I want to face the jury box, the court reporter is often behind me. That is a problem. My immediate concern is that I need to convince these people sitting in front of me, the jury. I want to make meaningful, authentic contact. My second concern is making sure the court reporter gets every word. Rena's exercise of Radiating 360 Degrees and filling the space can be really helpful in this regard.

There is a podium in every courtroom. Sometimes its use is mandated. Supreme Court and Appellate arguments are delivered from behind podiums. Sometimes it's expected, but always it is just there. If it is there, people tend to use them. I advise against it. It is an energy block. Unless the Court absolutely insists, I don't do it. I am 5 feet 2 inches tall, so all they see over the podium is my head. I can't make an intimate connection with the jury from behind a podium.

Sidebar

I pretend Oprah or some celebrity newsagent is interviewing me so I can promote my latest project. It helps me find the core of my case, and from there, I can identify a line of connection to my audience. If my "interview" turns into a lecture, then I start over. I keep going until I have a sound bite.

—Rebecca Newman, Attorney

Communicating with the Jury

As you will hear from Laurie and in the Sidebar from Lisa, Beverly, and Rebecca, the first point to observe when you are communicating with a jury is to be yourself. My goal in coaching is to help clients become the best version of themselves—grounded, centered, and connected to deep central breathing. Warm up the voice and body so that you arrive prepared. If it is a long day and you have a lunch break, warm up again and shake off any tension or frustration you picked up in the first half of the day.

Remember that the jury is always watching you, so you can never let down. Alignment must stay strong and upright—not rigid. I use the term "relaxed readiness." My speech-language pathologist colleague

Joanna Cazden calls it "calm buzz," meaning you are excited and ready to do the task but you are calm and confident. If you have an expressive face that betrays you, put relaxing face muscles in your warm-up. By alternately opening the face wide and scrunching it up tight several times, the face muscles relax. Check in with the breath periodically throughout the day, relax the jaw, and your poker face will return. Pay attention to everything, listen and follow the action, and then you won't get a bored glaze that the jury will read at once. If you feel yourself being triggered, go into "slower, deeper, quieter, calmer" mode as you relax your shoulders. Pause before you respond. Don't do anything that will give the jury a reason to dislike you.

In Chapter 4, we talked about eye contact as it relates to body language. In this chapter, we mentioned it in the voir dire section. A number of the attorneys interviewed for this book emphasized the importance of eye contact. Make it a part of your everyday-at-the-office checklist.

Each time you speak in court, the jury hears you. Be aware of quality and tone of voice. You want your voice to be authoritative, confident, and warm, clear but easy on the ears. You now know that vocal quality is a controllable property of the voice (as are pitch variety, volume variety, and rate variety). You also know that the master keys for the expressive attorney are deep central breathing, accessing support, and making space in your mouth.

LAURIE

When communicating with the jury, authenticity is the rule of the day. If I don't believe something myself, then they are not going to believe it either. I can't persuade them to do something I don't believe. I approach it like we're friends and I am telling a compelling story about what happened and why it's their job to do something about it. That is far more effective than memorizing a long opening and delivering it to perfection—the Mr. Lawyer Suit again. You need to break through that barrier and become authentic. That's powerful, but it can take a lot of work.

Sidebar

Jurors do NOT want to be there. They are bored. It is like watching paint dry to them. I had a juror once who started snoring while a witness was testifying in a murder trial. Juries are shocked when there are no Perry Mason moments. They watch too much television and think that real court is like television. They want science in the courtroom that does not exist; but they saw it on television or on the Internet.

—Beverly Atteberry, Attorney

Friendliness with the jury will garner their patience and understanding. Addressing them with humility can help them feel at ease in an otherwise serious and stressful environment. Most jurors are first-timers and have no idea of what to expect. They are afraid of doing or saying the wrong thing. They want to impress, so let them. I try to be conscious of keeping my body language open and relaxed because if I am at ease, it conveys to an audience that maybe a potentially negative issue or statement isn't as important as opposing counsel implies.

I tell a story and I give the jury something to which they can attach memory. I walk in front of the jury box and use pauses to emphasize my points. I make eye contact with the jurors and purposefully nod my head up and down when I want them to agree; if they nod back, then I know that they are paying attention.

—Rebecca Newman, Attorney

Examining and Cross-Examining Witnesses

LAURIE

There are two different styles of examining witnesses: direct examination and cross-examination. For direct examination, I have had the opportunity to work with the witness before. The witness generally knows what I am going to ask. For cross-examination of a witness, I may not have met this person before—at least I haven't had a chance to work with them. We are in opposition and you have no idea how it is going to go. These roles feel very different from the get-go.

A trial is a play, and the person on the opposite side of this script may or may not be predictable. If I am examining my own witnesses, I have run over the script with them. They know what's coming, and I know what they are going to say. With an opposing witness, I have my script, but I have no idea what is going to come out of the witness's mouth. It is a kind of improv, a theatre game. You are thinking on your feet, controlling body language. I don't want the jury to know that what this guy just said totally threw me off my game; this could kill my case if I don't handle it right. Part of the challenge when you are cross-examining and have so much going in your head is that you can forget there is someone watching—the jury—and they are the most important element.

When I am doing a direct examination of a witness, I usually want the jurors' focus on this witness. I would rather blend into the wallpaper and not even be there. The witness needs me to structure the story and often needs me for emotional support. In this case, my voice is more modulated, even but clear. But I don't want the jury to focus on me.

Cross-examination is a different ball game. I need to ask the questions the jury wants answered. A cross-examination can be antagonistic—not always, but it can be. I think that is an area where a female lawyer runs a risk of being perceived as a bitch. It's our job, it's what we are supposed to do; and yet societal expectations can penalize us for doing our jobs. Articles have been written about that based on research. I continue to practice Rena's power without press in order to find the balance between firm and authoritative versus shrill and aggressive.

When I stand up to do an opening or closing, I am aware that I am persuading and I focus on that job. When I am doing directs and cross, that is the secondary concern. My focus tends to be more on content. Are we meeting every requirement that I need to in order to prove our case? Or on the cross, am I making all the points I need to? For me, the presentation falls to the side—it is a much lower concern. Still you have all these other things that are competing for attention.

The voice and body work we have been practicing throughout this book is also valuable as you approach examining and cross-examining witnesses. As we have said, vocal flexibility means having easy control of all aspects of your voice, including tonal quality, volume level, pitch and rate variety, inflection, and emotional nuance. This vocal agility can help you on two crucial fronts:

- Getting the responses you need from the witness.
- Signposting for the jury the journey you are taking them on.

Now, of course, in the middle of an examination, you are not focused on how you are using voice and body language. You are listening so that you can pursue your objectives of getting the right response and signposting for the jury. Because you have trained, done the work, and warmed up, your voice is ready to authentically support whatever you need.

I would like to revisit the idea of using objectives and action verbs to simulate your imagination and thus stimulate vocal nuances. If you can clearly identify your objective or your need in simple terms of action verbs, your voice and body will follow. Do you need to coax the witness, to comfort, to scare, or to imprint on the jury? By giving yourself clear verb images your body and voice can help you by being more specific and authentic.

Authentic is the word, isn't it? Authenticity comes from where you focus your thought energy. If the need "to scare" is felt in your center, on the breath, the result will be authentic. If you are mentally manipulating and thinking about how you can say this to scare him, it will, in fact, sound phony and forced. This is the magic. You must truly believe; the need comes from a deep place of knowing and trusting that the breath will lead you to the truth. Attorneys find this challenging because they are used to leading with their intellects, with their heads.

Sidebar

So as you move forward in your career, your number one consideration is to be comfortable in your own skin. Part of what helps me is being ultra-prepared. I am completely anal. If you're fully prepared, you are more confident and calmer. You're always going to get curveballs; but if you are prepared, you can react calmly to them.

It's okay at times to get animated with a witness, especially if you feel fairly certain the witness is not being truthful or is sidestepping the issue. Sometimes you have to rein them in a little bit, but always in a respectful way. If you start battling with someone on their turf, you're going to lose. And even if you never get the answer, as long as you maintain your position with steady confidence and respectfulness, the jury will get the message. They know the witness isn't answering the question. You need to pick your spots to lift the voice a little, maybe step a little closer, move around. But you don't want to be a distraction.

—Lisa Riggs, Attorney

We owe a debt to the women who came before us in this profession. I am friends with women who graduated from law school in the 1970s who felt like they had to act like men in order to be successful. But I haven't had to do that. I have always gotten to simply be myself. I recognize how fortunate I am. I know that the reason I get to be "real" is because of all the women who came before me who worked exceptionally hard to help male lawyers become comfortable with women in the courtroom, in boardrooms, in the classroom, and in the conference room. I am incredibly grateful to those women.

—Laura Clark Fey

We have covered a lot of ground in this book. Laurie and I wanted to create a process that will lead to true transformation. We are both committed to the empowerment of women. Laurie, through her law practice and in teaching women attorneys to own their power, has become a change agent in her field. I, through my work as a voice and presentation coach for women attorneys, seek to enhance a woman's effectiveness whenever she communicates. Women are uniquely suited to be medicine in our troubled world. By the nature of our genetics, our innate compassion, and our ability to work collaboratively, we are situated to change the world. The better we communicate, the more we enhance our other skills to support this huge task. We must be in it for the long haul, and we know that the short term may sometimes be frustrating, challenging, and often disappointing. But we can and we must become all that we are capable of. It only takes practice!

Sidebar Biographies

Gale Allison, JD, LLM, AEP®, has four decades of estate, trust, and tax experience as an estate and trust lawyer, litigator, and consultant on related tax issues. Three mediation certifications include family and divorce (The Mediation Institute), litigation, and elder care (Pepperdine, Straus Institute). Before entering private practice, she was a litigator for the federal government and an estate and gift tax attorney for the Internal Revenue Service. A member of the Tennessee, Georgia, and Oklahoma bar associations and the American Bar Association, she is currently an attorney/director at Schaffer Herring, PLLC, and mediates exclusively through Dispute Resolution Consultants in Tulsa.

Beverly Atteberry is a graduate of Saint Gregory's College (A.S), Oklahoma Baptist University (B.A.), and the University of Tulsa College of Law (J.D.). She has been a jury trial attorney for more than twenty-seven years and a solo practitioner for the past twenty-two years. She was born and raised in Blackwell, Oklahoma, to a farming family with a strong reverence for education and community involvement. She is an eight-plus-gallon blood donor, a member and officer of many organizations including Metro Tulsa Career & Professional Women, Oklahoma Steam Threshers & Gas Engine Association, Republican Women's Club of Tulsa County, Tulsa Hope Academy, Catholic Business & Professional Women, and Quota. She is a member of the Church of Saint Mary's and enjoys traveling, reading, scrapbooking, crocheting, gardening, and quilting.

Teri Aulph entered the corporate world in the middle of her career and within three years rose to the level of executive in the automotive industry, followed by an executive position in various Fortune 500 companies. Now as an author, speaker, executive coach, and business consultant globally, she helps companies capitalize on their biggest asset: their people—talent management and people solutions.

Shena Burgess is a partner at Smiling, Smiling & Burgess practicing insurance and criminal defense. She graduated from the University of Tulsa College of Law and immediately began working as a Tulsa County Public Defender, rising to Deputy Chief. She is an adjunct professor at the University of Tulsa teaching Trial Skills and coaching the American Association of Justice Trial Team. She has been awarded the following: Excellence in Coaching Award, Outstanding Adjunct Professor, Metro Tulsa Business Professional Women's Young Carecrist of the Year, Tulsa Women Lawyer's Association as one of Outstanding Women Lawyers, Fern Holland Award, and the President's Award.

Felicia Collins Correia served in nonprofit executive leadership roles for over twenty-five years as CEO of Domestic Violence Intervention Services/Call Rape and the YWCA Tulsa. She oversaw two successful nonprofit mergers and was instrumental in creating systemic change with Tulsa Law Enforcement (Police, Sheriff, District Attorney) and with the Judiciary, for which she received numerous awards in recognition of this work. She is now a consultant specializing in professionalizing nonprofits, analyzing organizational and infrastructure gaps, and transforming staff and organizational culture.

Stephanie Duran is an Associate in the Tulsa office of GableGotwals. Her focus is on helping employers proactively comply with labor and employment laws and defending employers in labor and employment litigation, arbitration, and administrative proceedings. Formerly an Assistant District Attorney for Tulsa County, she prosecuted domestic violence and harassment against women cases, winning guilty verdicts in every case she tried. Stephanie has successfully capitalized on her native Hispanic background and fluency in Spanish to work with non-English speaking parties, witnesses, managers, and supervisors. She also provides harassment, discrimination, and retaliation prevention training and education. She has volunteered for the National System for Integral Family Development, in Sinaloa, Mexico; and completed a Poverty Field Study in Bangalore, India, with the University Studies Abroad Consortium. She is currently serving as a Board Member of the Tulsa Global Alliance.

Valerie J. Evans is in general practice, with a primary emphasis in the area of Workers Compensation. She obtained her undergraduate degree in Political Science and her Juris Doctorate from the University of Oklahoma. Ms. Evans is a retired Major from the Oklahoma Army National Guard, having served in various positions including the Brigade Postal Officer, a Reserve Forces Officer of the Selective Service System, Inspector General, and S-1. She was admitted into the Oklahoma Bar Association and licensed to practice before the U.S. District Court of the Northern District of Oklahoma. She is married, a mother of two, and a grandmother of six amazing grandchildren.

Anna Fearheiley is a Regional Manager with iD Tech Camps, where she oversees technology education programs throughout New England. Her work includes training and coaching educators, empowering students, and managing logistics. In addition, Anna is the Managing Director of the Sanguine Theatre Company, a nonprofit organization in New York City focused on new plays. She is a University of Oklahoma graduate and one of Rena Cook's former students and assistants.

Laura Clark Fey, one of the first twenty-seven U.S. attorneys recognized as Privacy Law Specialists through the International Association of Privacy Professionals (IAPP), leads Fey LLC, a global data privacy and information governance law firm. She and her team help organizations develop and implement practical solutions to their unique data privacy and information governance challenges. Laura is a member of the inaugural class of IAPP Fellows of Information Privacy (FIP), a Certified U.S. and European Information Privacy Professional (CIPP/US/E), and a Certified Information Privacy Manager (CIPM). The U.S. Department of Commerce and the European Commission have selected Laura as an arbitrator in connection with the EU-U.S. Privacy Shield Framework Binding Arbitration Program. Laura has been selected into Baylor Law School's Brain Trust as a data privacy thought leader for its LLM in Litigation Management Program. She teaches Global Data Protection and Privacy Law at the University of Kansas School of Law.

Aurora Gregory is a marketer, author, and speaker. Some of the biggest brands in business have worked with her to get their messages right, create communications programs that connect with target audiences, and set marketing strategies that deliver results. Aurora has received accolades as a communications trainer, helping those with something to say develop skills to deliver their most important messages to customers, media, and presentation audiences. She has years of experience in leading speaker's bureau programs that have placed hundreds of speakers at local, national, and international conferences. She's passionate about coaching entrepreneurs on how to build meaningful connections with their customers so that they can grow their businesses.

Brittany Littleton is an experienced estate-planning and business-transactions attorney. She owns and operates Littleton Legal PLLC, a boutique law firm based in the Tulsa, Oklahoma, metropolitan area. Her practice focuses on estate planning, elder law, trust and probate administration, business law, and outside general counsel services for closely held companies. Brittany is an active supporter of entrepreneurs in her community. She is often invited to speak to business owners about planning strategies that mitigate risk and empower businesses to thrive. She serves on the executive board for her local chamber of commerce. Brittany is also a social justice advocate and a board member at her local YWCA. She believes that empowering women to bravely stand in their power is a critical element of eliminating discrimination, racism, and economic injustice on a broader scale.

Ellen McClure is Associate Professor of French and History at the University of Illinois-Chicago, where she has also served as Head of the Department of French and Francophone Studies. She is currently the Associate Director of the School of Literatures, Cultural Studies, and Linguistics. She has also been directing the university's program in Religious Studies. She is the author of *Sunspots and the Sun King: Sovereignty and Mediation in Seventeenth-Century France* and soon to be published *The Logic of Idolatry: Creation, Authorship, and the Will in Seventeenth-Century France.* In her spare time, she serves as an ordained Zen Buddhist lay teacher at the Zen Buddhist Temple in Chicago.

Diana Morgan is a Life Coach, a Certified EFT (Emotional Freedom Technique) Practitioner, and a Matrix Reimprinting Practitioner. Both EFT and Matrix Reimprinting are powerful techniques designed to help people release stuck patterns and traumas so that they can attain their goals and find peace and happiness. Diana is the founder of Alchemy of Change, LLC. She holds a master's degree in Counseling Psychology from Boston College and is a Certified Clinical Herbalist and Nutritionist as well as a Massage Therapist. She is passionate about natural healing in all its forms. The primary aspiration in her career is to help people to be happy and healthy and to follow their dreams.

Rebecca L. Newman is a Senior Associate and trial attorney at Rhodes Hieronymus in Tulsa, Oklahoma. Her practice centers on civil litigation with an emphasis on commercial, transportation, and insurance matters. Ms. Newman began her practice in 2012 as a solo practitioner and has a range of experience, including criminal defense. Her key presentation is on the utilization of Fifth Amendment Privilege in overlapping civil and criminal defense cases.

Cheena Pazzo is a partner in Kanati Strategies specializing in integrated marketing, communications, and business operations. She has worked with major corporations, nonprofit organizations, health care companies, and trade associations and has also focused on government issues. She executes large-scale campaigns and provides consulting services for business operations, organizational assessments, and issues management. She previously served as a Vice President of Marketing and Communications for the nation's largest nonprofit health care organization where she launched national strategic directives in market, expanding online presence and growing market share through highly targeted outreach. She is also an experienced crisis communicator with a background in transition management, mergers and acquisitions, and litigation communications.

E. Kathleen Pence was born and raised in Tulsa, Oklahoma, and chose to build her law practice in her hometown. Ms. Pence attended the University of Tulsa for her undergraduate degree and returned to the University of Tulsa College of Law to obtain her Juris Doctorate in 2011. Ms. Pence has numerous and varied experiences in the legal field from working for multiple judges at the Tulsa County Courthouse prior to attending law school to working in a medium-sized insurance defense firm, striking out on her own in 2012 to form a small law firm. Ms. Pence then founded Pence Law Firm as a solo practitioner, which opened its doors on January 1, 2016. Ms. Pence serves on several boards, including the Small Business Connection Advisory Board and the South Tulsa Community Housing Board. She was chosen from applicants throughout the state of Oklahoma to participate in the Oklahoma Leadership Academy for the Oklahoma Bar Association as a rising leader in the legal profession. In addition to her passion for the legal community, Ms. Pence has a love for the fine arts. As a lifelong musician, Ms. Pence obtained her undergraduate degree in music and is still involved in the arts community.

Jenny Proehl-Day is a practicing attorney in Tulsa, Oklahoma. She grew up in rural Minnesota and dreamed of becoming an attorney and changing the world. She moved to Tulsa, Oklahoma, in 2000 to attend the University of Tulsa and the College of Law. She is a first-generation college graduate, and in 2011 she was sworn into the Oklahoma Bar. She practices criminal defense, family law, and civil rights violations. While she hasn't changed the world yet, she has succeeded in breaking glass ceilings as the first female candidate to run for Tulsa County District Attorney. Jenny is married and has two daughters.

Lisa Riggs is a managing partner at Riggs, Abney, Neal, Turpen, Orbison, & Lewis, with offices in Tulsa, Oklahoma City, and Denver, Colorado. Lisa is a civil trial lawyer, a member of the American Association for Justice and the Oklahoma Association for Justice, and has devoted her career representing victims of substandard medical care, faulty products, unsafe medical and pharmaceutical products, and other life-altering and life-threatening conditions and situations. She was a partner at her law firm in Washington, DC, before moving back home to Oklahoma in 1996. Lisa serves on many community boards and volunteer organizations. She is an AV Preeminent rated attorney and has been recognized as one of the Top Attorneys in Oklahoma.

Esther M. Sanders was born in the small town of Macks Creek, Missouri. She graduated from Drury College in Springfield, Missouri, with a Bachelor of Science in Criminal Justice. She attended Oklahoma City University where she received her Juris Doctor degree in law in December 1992. After working for a firm in Oklahoma City for two years, Esther opened her own practice, Sanders & Associates, P.C. law office, in Tulsa, Oklahoma, on January 2, 1995. Esther continues to represent injured people seeking recovery in civil court, workers' compensation court, and social security disability benefits.

Kathy Taylor is a tireless advocate and change agent for Tulsa. She was elected Mayor of Tulsa, Oklahoma, in 2006, seeing the city through its worst recession in seventy years. She is currently Chief of Economic Development in the Office of Tulsa's Mayor, G. T. Bynum. She has also served as Oklahoma Secretary of Commerce and Tourism as well as Chief of Education Strategy and Innovation. She serves on the Board of Directors of Sonic Industries, Chair of the Leadership Council for ImpactTulsa, and is a regional board member of Reading Partners. Through the Lobeck Taylor Family Foundation she works to stay at the forefront of innovation and is a collaborator in Tulsa's entrepreneurial ecosystem.

Endnotes

1. Christine K. Jahnke, *The Well Spoken Women: Your Guide to Looking and Sounding Your Best* (Amherst, MA: Prometheus Books, 2011).
2. Lara Bazelon, "What It Takes to Become a Trial Attorney If You Are Not a Man," *The Atlantic*, September 2018.
3. NYSBA, "If Not Now, When? Achieving Equality for Women Attorneys in the Courtroom and ADR," November 2017.
4. Sue Shellenbarger, "Is This How You Really Talk?" *Wall Street Journal*, April 23, 2013.
5. Bazelon, "What It Takes to Become a Trial Attorney."
6. Ibid.
7. Carol Gilligan, *In a Different Voice* (Cambridge, MA: Harvard University Press, 2009).
8. The terms "Denial" and "Bluff" are adapted from Patsy Rodenburg, *The Actor Speaks* (New York: Palgrave Macmillan, 2002).
9. Adam Bryant, "Knowing, as a Leader, When to Let Go," *Wall Street Journal*, April 23, 2017.
10. Jahnke, *The Well Spoken Women*.
11. Bazelon, "What It Takes to Become a Trial Attorney."
12. Sheryl Sandburg, *Lean In: Women, Work, and the Will to Lead* (New York: Knopf, 2013).
13. Dennis Lewis, *The Tao of Natural Breathing* (San Francisco: Mountain Wind Publishing, 1997).
14. David Carey, "The Responsive Breath," in *Breath in Action: The Art of Breath in Vocal and Holistic Practice*, Eds. Jane Boston and Rena Cook (London: Jessica Kingsley Publishers, 2009).
15. Patsy Rodenburg, *The Actor Speaks* (New York: Palgrave Macmillan, 2002).
16. Sylvia Ann Hewlett, *Executive Presence: The Missing Link Between Merit and Success* (New York: HarperCollins, 2014).
17. Kristi Hedges, *The Power of Executive Presence: Unlock Your Potential to Influence and Engage Others* (New York: AMACOM, 2012).

18. Kate DeVore and Starr Cookman, *The Voice Book: Caring for, Protecting, and Improving Your Voice* (Chicago: Chicago Review Press, 2009).
19. Sylvia Ann Hewlett, *Executive Presence: The Missing Link Between Merit and Success* (New York: HarperCollins, 2014).
20. Felicia Collins Correia, Interview, June 13, 2017.
21. Rodenburg, *The Actor Speaks*.
22. Caroline Goyder, *Gravitas: Communicate with Confidence, Influence and Authority* (London: Random House, 2014).
23. Meribeth Dayme, *Presence, Confidence, and Personal Power* (Pennsauken, NJ: BookBaby, 2014).
24. Diana Morgan, Confidence and Presence Seminar, February 2, 2017.
25. Katty Kay and Claire Shipman, *The Confidence Code: The Science and Art of Self Assurance* (New York: HarperCollins, 2014).
26. Andrew Weil, *Breath: The Master Key to Self-Healing* (Watertown, CT: Thorne Communications, 1999).
27. Lexlee Overton, Email Interview, August 21, 2019, www.mindoverlaw.com.
28. Hewlett, *Executive Presence.*
29. Dayme, *Presence, Confidence and Personal Power*.
30. Google, Accessed July 17, 2019, https://en.wikipedia.org/wiki/suspense.
31. David Ball and Joshua Karton, *Theatre for Trial*, Trial Guides, LLC, 2017.
32. Rebecca Diaz-Bonilla, *Foolproof: An Attorney's Guide to Oral Communication* (Boulder, CO: NITA, 2014).
33. Hedges, *The Power of Executive Presence*.
34. Google, "Why Michelle Obama Is a Great Speaker," accessed May 1, 2017, from http://www.stalwartcom.com/blog/why-michelle-obama-is-a-great-speaker.
35. Google, Vanessa Van Edwards, "The Science of People," accessed August 10, 2019, from https://www.scienceofpeople.com/.
36. Robert Johnson, Bold Networking, https://www.boldnetworking.com.
37. Google, Edwards, "The Science of People."
38. Google, Eric Berne, "Transactional Analysis and Ego States," accessed August 18, 2019, from https://ericberne.com/transacational-analysis/.
39. Marshall Rosenberg, *Non Violent Communication: A Language of Life* (Encinitas, CA: Puddle Dancer, 2005).
40. Ed Brodow, *Negotiation Boot Camp* (New York: Currency Doubleday, 2006).
41. Ibid.
42. Ball and Karton, *Theatre for Trial*.

Index